Being tried and tested changes your outlook on life. You no longer take things for granted: a hug, a meal with those you love, companionship. Thank you, Robert, for encouraging us to see every day and every blessing as a precious treasure. Thank you for the motivation you've given us to live our lives to the fullest with no regrets.
—Gracia Burnham, New Tribes Mission,
Author of *In the Presence of My Enemies*

Life is fragile, and our hopes and dreams can be shattered in the blink of an eye. The only thing left is God. This compelling true story displays God's faithfulness even in the face of devastating loss. Robert is a living example of how God takes great tragedy and uses it for something wonderful.
—C. Thomas Davis, President of Children's HopeChest

When we are thrust into catastrophic tragedy, God magnificently holds on to us. I discovered this through the loss of my husband on the space shuttle *Columbia*, and Robert has discovered this through the extreme loss of his wife and children. This book shouts from the mountaintops of God's faithfulness in our every trial and tribulation.
—Evelyn Husband, Author of *High Calling: The Courageous Life and Faith of Space Shuttle* Columbia *Commander Rick Husband*

Bad things can happen to good people. The true quality of character is seen when a person faces great tragedy and personal loss. Robert Rogers is a great man with a good education, awesome talent, a beautiful personality, and, most importantly, he is an anointed man of God. By the grace of God, he has overcome one of life's greatest tragedies in the loss of his wife and all four of his children. Robert's love for God and his close personal relationship with Jesus

have given him strength not only to overcome but to minister strength to others who might encounter tragedies and hardships.
—Dr. Ron Kenoly, Worship Leader and Conference Speaker

After reading *Into the Deep,* I found myself thanking God, first for His goodness; second, for Robert's story; and third, for my family. We owe Robert a debt of gratitude for his willingness to revisit the excruciating loss of his wife and children in order to share with us the divine grace that sustains and mends our broken hearts. In the drama and heartache of a real-life tragedy, *Into the Deep* recounts a victorious journey through the valley of the shadow of death by relying on the companionship of God. We learn from Robert that Christians do indeed grieve, but as Saint Paul said, not like those who have no hope.
—Chuck Smith, Jr., Author of *There Is a Season*
and *Frequently Avoided Questions*

Robert Rogers is a man of many sorrows, and yet those who hear his story will experience genuine hope and deep joy that defy explanation. *Into the Deep* will challenge your suppositions, expand your faith, and stretch your heartstrings.
—Kathy Troccoli, Recording Artist, Author

Robert Rogers's faith in unspeakable loss leaves me humbled and silenced. It does not reflect the tragedy in his life but the greatness of God and His unwavering mercies and grace.
—Donna VanLiere, *New York Times* bestselling author
of *The Christmas Shoes* and *The Angels of Morgan Hill*

Be prepared to be forever impacted by *Into the Deep.*
—Dr. Joe White, President of Kanakuk Kamps

one man's story

of how tragedy

took his family

but could not

take his faith

Into the Deep

robert rogers

with **stan finger**

foreword by **nancy guthrie**

Tyndale House Publishers, Inc.
Carol Stream, Illinois

A Focus on the Family book published by
Tyndale House Publishers, Carol Stream, Illinois 60188

Focus on the Family and the accompanying logo and design are federally registered trademarks of Focus on the Family, Colorado Springs, CO 80995.

TYNDALE and Tyndale's quill logo are registered trademarks of Tyndale House Publishers, Inc.

Editor: Brandy Bruce
AD/Designer: Joseph Sapulich
Cover photo of water copyright © by Veer. All rights reserved.
Family cover photo taken by Robert Rogers.
Robert Rogers author photo: Sunflower Studio Photography by Tracy Dohm

Library of Congress Cataloging-in-Publication Data
Rogers, Robert, 1966-
  Into the deep / by Robert Rogers with Stan Finger.
     p. cm.
  ISBN: 978-1-58997-378-7
  1. Rogers, Robert, 1966- 2. Spiritual biography—Kansas. 3. Consolation. 4. Suffering—Religious aspects—Christianity. 5. Disasters—Religious aspects—Christianity. 6. Floods—Kansas. I. Finger, Stan. II. Title.
  BR1725.R635A3 2007
  248.8'66092—dc22
  [B]

                                                            2006037374

Printed in the United States of America
12 13 14 / 16

Contents

Foreword

I 'll never forget flipping the television channels past CNN and seeing Robert Rogers speaking at a press conference on September 1, 2003. Much of what he said had been edited out for the news report, but no producer could edit out his peaceful countenance and obvious inner strength at what was the lowest moment of his life. *That is a man of faith,* I remember thinking, even as I tried to keep myself from imagining what it must feel like to lose your entire family, to be the only survivor, so alone, and so desperately sad.

It was just a couple of months later that Robert made a trip to Nashville, and through mutual friends we connected for a long breakfast of eggs and toast and shared sorrow. He opened up to my husband, David, and me the excruciating details you'll read in this account of that stormy night. My face grimaced and my eyes closed as I got a taste of the pain of that terrible night, the agony of its realities. Robert showed us beautiful pictures of his beloved Melissa and happy children and we felt with him the intense loneliness of his empty home.

I was struck not only by his sorrow but also by his softness, his passionate love for his family, and his palpable love for God. At one point, after more than one verse of Scripture flowed naturally off his lips and into our conversation, I asked him, "Robert, how do you have so much Scripture memorized?"

He explained to me that he discovered Scripture memory as a Catholic high-school student who was hungry to know God by knowing His Word. But his love affair with Scripture didn't end there. He lovingly remembered all the bedtimes spent with his children, memorizing Scripture together. "By the time she was five, our daughter

Makenah could quote Psalm 121: 'I lift up my eyes to the hills—where does my help come from? My help comes from the LORD, the Maker of heaven and earth,' " he told us.

So it was only natural that in the most fearful moment of their lives, as the water rose in and around their van, they began to speak Scripture from Psalm 46: "God is our refuge and strength, an ever-present help in trouble. Therefore we will not fear . . ." (verses 1–2). God continues to be an ever-present help, rescuing Robert daily from despair as he clings to the promises of God and finds his refuge in God.

If you have wondered whether God will live up to His promises if the worst thing you can imagine happens to you, Robert's story will show you what God's faithfulness looks like. And if you have ever wondered if you will be able to survive and keep living if you lose those who are most precious to you, Robert will show you what it looks like to trust God wholeheartedly, what it feels like to reach out and find God's presence there as He walks with you—into the deep.

—Nancy Guthrie
Author of *Holding on to Hope*

Acknowledgments

I first acknowledge Jesus as my sole Savior, my sole Provider, my sole Redeemer, and my sole Healer. His grace sustained me through the fiercest storm. God—and God alone—is my strength. I live to worship Him and know Him.

"I want to know Christ and the power of his resurrection and the fellowship of sharing in his sufferings" (Philippians 3:10). More people have prayed for and influenced my life than I could ever acknowledge within this book—even more than I will ever know this side of heaven. Without each of you, I wouldn't be poised in this place to bring God even greater glory. I could never repay you for your selfless generosity. Only God knows all your names and deeds. I ask Him to bless you abundantly for your gifts of sacrifice.

Thank you . . . from the deepest corners of my life.

In Christ I remain,

Robert Rogers

I'd like to thank Robert for trusting me to help convey his story of love, loss, and faith. My family and friends supported me unwaveringly throughout this journey. And most of all, God has showered me with countless gifts and blessings. As I look back, I'm humbled to recognize how He prepared me for such a time as this—"Yet who knows whether you have come to the kingdom for such a time as this?" (Esther 4:14, NKJV).

—Stan Finger

Prologue

T he dark cloud came up in the morning. By 10 A.M. on May 6, 1886, it was raining so hard in the Flint Hills of Kansas that one resident said water "ran over the yard like oil."

Within an hour, Jacob Creek had overflowed and was flooding nearby fields.

Benjamin Jacobs lived on the banks of the creek with his young family, and he grew concerned as the rain kept falling and the creek kept rising. He hitched a mule team to a large wagon and loaded his wife, two children, and brother aboard.

He began driving toward higher ground, through water that was already several inches deep and still rising. He had taken a shortcut through a cornfield and was approaching a hill when a huge wave bore down on them.[1]

"When I looked up on the creek," he said later, "the waves were rolling over and over much higher than the wagon."

It looked, one witness said, like "a great wall of water."

The wave capsized the wagon and drowned the mules. Benjamin Jacobs managed to grab hold of a limb in a tree that was all but covered by the raging floodwaters. His brother, William, grabbed a tree limb with one hand and Ben's seven-year-old son with the other, and they climbed to safety.

But Jacobs' wife, Martha, and his infant daughter, Edna May, were swept away to their deaths. Edna May was found just a few hours later, but it took searchers three days to find Martha. They were buried in a cemetery overlooking the prairie that had been their home.[2]

Jacob Creek slipped back into silence for more than 100 years. But on a dark summer's night in 2003, a wall of water would strike again.

Deep calls to deep in the roar of your waterfalls;
all your waves and breakers have swept over me.
—PSALM 42:7

1

"It's Friday!"

Enjoying. Paying attention.
No hurry to get on to something more important.
Whatever we are doing is important,
experiencing each moment along the way.
Time is a gift.
—Poem displayed in Robert and Melissa Rogers's home

I pulled into the garage of our one-and-a-half-story Cape Cod home in the Kansas City suburb of Liberty, Missouri, walked through the door into our kitchen, and made an announcement.

"It's Frrrrriiiidaaaaaaaay!"

My wife, Melissa, and our four children greeted those words with spontaneous cheers, and I was quickly tackled by my two boys.

Melissa and I loved taking ordinary moments and making them special for our family, whether it was baking a batch of cookies, carving a pumpkin, or cheering because the weekend had arrived.

"Let's make a memory!" Melissa often said.

This Friday of Labor Day weekend 2003 would offer a lasting

one. We often held "Family Fun Night" on Fridays. For us, that meant popcorn, pizza, movies, and ice cream.

"Who wants to go with Daddy to get some movies?" I asked.

Before I could finish the whole sentence, I heard two voices offer a resounding "Me!"—Makenah Alexandra, our eight-year-old daughter, and Nicholas Adam, our three-year-old son. Alenah WenYing, our 21-month-old special-needs daughter whom we had just adopted in January, had a caught-off-guard expression on her face, as if she sensed she had just missed out on an important vote.

I also deciphered an enthusiastic grunting yell of approval from Zachary Seth, who was diagnosed with Down syndrome the day after his birth nearly six years earlier. He had a cleft palate, so he had a very limited spoken vocabulary.

Melissa wanted to feed Alenah and bake one of her scrumptious tomato, pepperoni, and mushroom pizzas while we were gone. So I packed our three oldest children into the van and drove to the local grocery store to pick up a few necessities and rent a couple of movies.

When we returned home, the fabulous fragrance of homemade pizza greeted us at the door.

"Hooray!" Melissa cheered as we piled into the kitchen.

My wife had been a cheerleader in high school and was still a perpetual encourager to others—always bubbly and cheerful wherever she went. Her radiant, captivating smile had captured my heart more than 13 years earlier at a sidewalk café in downtown Boston, Massachusetts.

I helped our oldest children wash their hands, and they took their spot on the white bedsheet that Melissa had spread out on the floor in front of the television. Melissa settled Alenah in her high chair where she could munch on pizza bites without being pestered by the boys.

"Let's pray!" I said.

Prayer time and talking to Jesus was as normal for us as breathing. Melissa and I made a conscious effort to show our relationship with God to our children every day, not just relegate it to once a week on Sunday mornings. We would often say "Thank You, Jesus," for simple little things around the house or surprises along the way. We would frequently pray out loud for somebody's ouchie or for an ambulance that went by.

We held hands and said our standard mealtime prayer, ending with a strong *Aaaaaaaaaaaaaaa-men!*

All our children, especially Zachary, would chime in loudly on the "Amen," not just with their voices, but also with their hands using sign language. It was our trademark punctuation on the prayer, but it was also a release word: Now it was okay to dive into dinner!

After pizza, a bag of popcorn, and two short episodes of *Scooby-Doo,* it was getting late.

"Okay—time for bed!" I announced as I turned off the TV.

"Aaaawwwwww!" Makenah whined.

None of us wanted the fun part of the evening to be over so soon, but Saturday was a big day. We would be driving 200 miles to Wichita, Kansas, for Melissa's Uncle Mark's wedding. Still, I couldn't resist sneaking in a little bit of music time around my grandmother's Steinway baby-grand piano before heading to bed. I started playing a ragtime piece, and Makenah threw the cushions from the sofa onto the floor so that she and the others could bounce up and down.

This was the kind of night we loved—just us and our kids enjoying genuine fun and laughter together. I played two more songs, and then we ushered all four children upstairs to get them ready for bed.

Our bedtime ritual included prayer and Scripture memorization. Years before, we had heeded the advice we heard from Dr. Joe White on a Focus on the Family radio broadcast to teach your children Scripture every night before going to sleep.

Melissa and I took turns tucking each child into bed. Before I slipped out of Makenah's room, I placed my hand on her forehead and said, "May the Lord bless you, heal you, keep you, and protect you. May He make His face shine upon you and give you peace and favor all the days of your life. In Jesus' name, Amen."

It was a blessing I gave to all our children almost every night.

With the kids in bed, Melissa and I prepared all the necessities for the long trip awaiting us in the morning: diaper bags, snacks, toys, tapes of Focus on the Family's *Adventures in Odyssey*, extra clothes, pillows, and blankets for the ride home. We wrapped the wedding presents and packed the van as best we could until morning.

We were ready to call it a night, but not before Melissa and I each had a bowl of ice cream as we sat on the couch, taking time to talk about our day. When it was time for bed, we headed to the living room, where we'd set up our bed while we were remodeling our upstairs bedroom.

"I love you," I said, like every other night, kissing Melissa gently on the lips.

"I love you, too," she replied, after returning my peck.

We drifted off into a deep sleep and didn't stir until the alarm clock woke us the next morning.

Since neither of us were "morning" people, Melissa and I would typically hit the snooze cycle on the alarm clock. But not this morning. The wedding was at 1:00 in Wichita, a good three-hour drive from Kansas City. Because I was an usher for the wedding, we had to arrive by 11:30 A.M. We also wanted to allow time to change our kids' clothes and give Matt, Melissa's brother, time to change into the suit Melissa had just bought for him.

Even though we would be somewhat crunched for time, I still wanted to cook "Daddy's Famous Flapjacks" for breakfast. Our kids loved pancakes, and this was a tradition we kept alive nearly every Saturday morning at home.

"Who wants to help Daddy make pancakes?" I asked.

"Meeee!" Nicholas volunteered.

I loved involving the children in anything I was doing, whether it was a trip to the hardware store, changing the oil, or, in this case, making pancakes. We finished stirring the batter, and I started making the pancakes. Melissa had Makenah and Zachary help set the table. We always preferred to have our kids help as much as possible with the meal preparations so they didn't get used to us just "waiting" on them.

While the last batch cooked, I sat down so we could say our mealtime prayer. I closed our prayer with a short postscript that my father had taught me years before as he prayed over our family of 10—Mom, Dad, and eight children, with me as the youngest—whenever we went on family vacations:

"Jesus, please grant that we may have a safe journey today, with no mishaps whatsoever, involving us or other people, our vehicle or the vehicles of others, our property or the property of others. We ask this in Your holy name so that we and others may always and better serve in Your holy name and for Your greater honor and glory. Your kingdom come, Your will be done. In Jesus' name, Amen."

We dove into breakfast, passing the syrup, cutting our children's pancakes, passing and spreading the butter. We chatted and laughed as we did every Saturday morning.

Time was short, so we cleaned up the kitchen and changed everyone into his or her traveling clothes. We knew better than to dress in our wedding clothes so many hours before the main event. Then we piled everyone into the van. Melissa wanted to drive first; she was usually the best one at getting us somewhere safely and in a hurry. But halfway down the street, we realized that we had forgotten the wedding presents!

"Arghhhh. I can't stand that!" Melissa groaned in frustration.

She spun us around and zipped back home. I ran in through the garage door, grabbed the presents, and gave the kitchen one last look. I didn't spot a small backpack just beyond the step into the family room. I returned to the van with the gifts.

"Got 'em. Let's go."

Rain fell steadily the entire drive to Wichita, but it was not enough to slow us down significantly. Melissa and I switched places about halfway, near Emporia, Kansas. Once we reached Wichita, we found the church on Woodlawn Avenue in plenty of time.

"Here we are, you guys!" I announced to everyone in the van as we arrived.

Melissa hopped out into the now pouring rain and rolled open the sliding door. I grabbed the umbrella and ran inside to find Matt and give him his suit. We were both ushers and needed to learn the seating instructions for the guests. When I returned to the van, Melissa had a frustrated look on her face.

"What's the matter?" I asked. "Anything I can do to help?"

"Oh, I'm so mad. I can't find the boys' bag of socks and spare clothes. I know I packed them, but I can't find them anywhere. I can't send our kids into the wedding in their nice clothes without socks! I bet we forgot the bag."

"We had a million and one details to remember. So what if they don't have socks. They're kids!"

Melissa was nevertheless agitated and frustrated with herself. She had a degree in interior design. The meticulous nature that flourished in design work could be a burden for her in other areas of her life. She liked everything to be just right.

The mini-crisis behind us, we finished juggling umbrellas, diapers, clothes, and children, and we all made our way through the rain into the church. After ushering guests to their seats, I joined my family in a row near the back. When the wedding ended, we filed out of the sanctuary and headed over to the church's reception hall. Cake, peanuts, and finger foods filled the tables. We gathered around a big table, along with Grandpa Jere, Melissa's dad, and Grandma Judy, Melissa's stepmom, plus Matt and his wife and four children. Many friends and relatives came up to meet our growing family and catch up on the latest developments.

Melissa seemed to glow. She was beaming from ear to ear, so happy with life and proud of our family of six. Many of our relatives had not yet met Alenah. Our children were busy playing hide-and-seek with their cousins, running around, and snatching snacks off the banquet tables. Zachary, who rarely wore shoes inside our home or outside in the backyard, had quickly discarded them and was running around barefoot.

We started taking portraits of various families in front of the food table. When it was our family's turn, we passed our camera around to relatives to capture the moment. Melissa, true to her daily mantra, wanted to "make a memory." She stood in front of the table with Makenah and Nicholas—one at each side, one in each arm. I snatched up Zachary and Alenah before they darted off again.

I knelt on my right knee and propped Zachary up on my left knee. He still had no shoes or socks on. I pulled Alenah in close to me and cupped her tiny tummy with my right hand. With my fingertips now under her arms, I squeezed and wiggled them ever so slightly to induce a smile for the picture. It worked, just as it had so many times in the past.

Amazingly, the picture turned out perfect: all six of us looking straight at the camera and smiling. That's a rare occurrence, as anyone with four small children knows.

It was 3:00 P.M.—almost time to bid the bride and groom farewell. But first we had to "dress" their car. Several of the men, including Melissa's dad and brother and me, went outside to complete the task. I brought Makenah along to witness the fun. She and I were on balloon duty, blowing them up and stuffing them into the car, while others draped streamers across the car and wrote "Just Married!" on the windows with soap. When we had all finished our handiwork, somebody drove the car around to the covered breezeway in anticipation of the newlyweds' departure.

We helped usher the bride and groom to their car in a flurry of laughs and cheers. They pulled balloons out of the way so they could climb in, and then they sped off. The kids played with the balloons for a while, and we took a few more photos. Then we brought our van around and loaded up the many presents that had piled up for the bride and groom. We followed the caravan of vehicles to the couple's house and carried the gifts into the living room.

After drying off and visiting for a few minutes around the

kitchen table, we asked, "Who wants to go have some ice cream with us at Braum's?"

Grandma and Grandpa, who typically jumped at any chance to have ice cream, gracefully declined so they could get back home at a decent time. But Melissa's brother, Matt, and his family accepted. We gave them directions to the store on Rock Road and agreed to meet there. We took our umbrellas and kids in hand and braved the rain.

By then, it was pouring again.

2

A Wall of Water

We considered the rain a blessing.

For two months, the Midwest had endured a lingering drought and searing temperatures. We were all praying for rain. Unfortunately, we got what we prayed for all at once. By 8:00 P.M. Saturday, the rain that had been falling almost nonstop for three days intensified into a virtual monsoon.

My family and I were eating ice cream with Melissa's brother and his family and talking away without noticing the clock. The eight kids from our two families had been playing on the slides for quite a while. Matt and his family had a solid three-hour drive to Hiawatha, Kansas, and we still faced a 200-mile drive of our own along the Kansas Turnpike back home to Liberty.

"Oh, my . . . look at the time," I remarked. "We'd better get moving."

All four parents got up from the table and began gathering everyone together. I grabbed the umbrella, went to the van, and retrieved the bag stuffed with all our children's jammies. We headed into the bathrooms—Melissa with the girls, me with the boys—and changed diapers and clothes one last time before our drive home.

We gathered with Matt's family by the entrance, lingering, taking a long time to hug and say good-bye.

Because it was raining so hard, we took turns with the oversized golf umbrella, escorting a few kids at a time to our minivans. I helped Melissa buckle and nestle all four kids into their special spots, making sure they each had a toy or two. Makenah was in the backseat, against the window on the driver's side. Zachary was next to her, near the sliding door. Alenah and Nicholas were in the middle bench, with Nicholas right next to the sliding door.

As I tucked in each one with their soft handmade quilts from Melissa's mom, I squeezed them and said to each by name, "I love you." Then I placed my hand on their foreheads and blessed them each with the prayer, "May the Lord bless you and heal you, keep you and protect you. May He make His face shine upon you and give you peace and favor, all the days of your life. Sweet dreams."

It's terribly tight for two adults to slide by each other inside a minivan full of kids. But Melissa and I had adapted very well to doing "gymnastics" in the van over the seats. I made my way into the driver's seat, and Melissa climbed into the passenger seat. I had driven this route home about once every three weeks for years as part of my job. We both buckled up, and as I pulled out of the parking lot, I tooted our horn as Matt and his family backed out.

I noticed our gas tank was less than half full. We would need more than that to get all the way home.

"We'd better fill up on gas before we leave," I told Melissa.

Better now in Wichita than later in Emporia, I figured. "I'm just going to swing by the gas pumps at Sam's," I said.

"Okay," Melissa answered, adding, "I think I'd like to drive first so I can sleep later. I'm up and ready to go now."

When Melissa was "on," she was "on"! But I still hoped to let her rest the entire way.

"I'm okay," I insisted. "I've driven this so many times. I can handle it myself."

It was shortly after 8:00 P.M., and the rain was pounding down on the roof of the gas station. A hard wind covered me with a misty spray. I finished filling up the gas tank and grabbed the receipt. I went to get in the driver's side, but Melissa had moved over and strapped herself into the seat.

"Too bad, bub," she declared. "I'm driving first."

"Okay," I replied, surrendering. "I'll try to rest while you drive."

I settled into the passenger seat. Melissa put the van into gear and headed north on Rock Road to K-254 East, which would take us to the Kansas Turnpike.

The children fell asleep soon after Melissa pulled onto the turnpike. I closed my eyes and tried to sleep so that Melissa and I could trade places somewhere on the other side of Emporia.

The rain refused to let up. In fact, it only got worse. I learned later that between 7:00 and 10:00 P.M., nearly seven inches of rain fell in the Jacob Creek watershed. At times during that period, the rain came down at the rate of five inches an hour. Our windshield wipers were on high speed, and Melissa was driving well below the speed limit, yet it was still difficult to see. At times, we couldn't see more than 25 feet in front of the minivan. It was terribly dark on this night—worse than I could ever remember it in this area. That's saying something, since there are no lights along this stretch of the Kansas Turnpike. Still, Melissa was an excellent and cautious driver.

There were other cars and trucks on the turnpike, so she knew to follow their taillights whenever possible.

The treacherous drive kept me awake, although I tried to close my eyes from time to time. Every now and then, I opened my eyes to check on Melissa and the driving conditions.

"Are you okay?" I asked.

"Yeah, I'm all right," she answered. "It's really bad out there, but I'm okay."

As I tried to sleep, I could hear the rhythm of the wipers on high speed: back-and-forth, back-and-forth, back-and-forth. Several times, my eyes shot open as I felt the van jerk suddenly to the left or right as Melissa maneuvered along the dark highway. At first, I was concerned that she was drifting to sleep and then suddenly awakening. But then I realized she was wide awake and simply trying to stay on the road.

Around 8:55 P.M., we saw several vehicles with their running lights still on scattered randomly along the right side of the road near milepost 116 in the Flint Hills. We assumed they had stopped because of the poor visibility and just wanted to sit out the storm. We didn't realize they had stopped because water was running over the highway. We couldn't see it. Everything looked black, except for the thick layer of mist that showed in our headlights as the rain pounded the pavement. Our minds were set on trying to keep our four children asleep and getting home as safely and as quickly as possible.

Since we didn't see any police, emergency vehicles, or yellow flashing Traffic Info signs, we didn't believe that I-35 had been shut down or that traffic was being redirected. There also wasn't any indication of an accident or injury. It appeared to us that the stopped vehicles were just waiting until the rain let up.

"Be careful of those cars over there," I cautioned.

"I know," Melissa said hesitantly. "Thanks. I'll keep following these ones."

We were among about eight vehicles that kept moving in the left lane past the stopped vehicles.

Almost instantly, it seemed as though we were surrounded by water—not just a pool, but a river flowing from right to left. We couldn't tell there was water on the road until the moment we were in it. The rain pounding on the pavement appeared the same as the rain falling on the flooded portion of the highway. In spite of the poor visibility, we could tell the water was up to our bumper already as our headlights beamed across the swelling current.

"Oh no! We're surrounded! What do we do?!" Melissa asked anxiously.

"Oh, God, help us!" I said in utter shock and disbelief.

We had never been in a flood, let alone a flash flood. All our senses were sharply on edge, trying to process every noise and move-ment—knowing the safety of our precious cargo, now fast asleep in their seats, was riding on our decisions. The whirl of the wind and the noise of the rain were so loud that it was hard to hear anything else. Wood debris floated rapidly across the highway. I could feel my heart pumping hard against my chest.

We saw taillights in front of us getting through.

"Let's keep following them," I suggested.

Melissa and I decided we should continue to drive through the water since we were already surrounded by it, and our van gave us more clearance above the highway than the cars already stopped along the edge. We figured that the height of the water was already at its worst.

Besides, we couldn't back up. We were boxed in. We had to go forward.

We knew, too, from firsthand experience in oceans, rivers, and riptides that even calf-high, rapidly moving water is dangerous to walk through and can knock you over. And we had four small children with us. It appeared to be several hundred feet to safe higher ground in either direction. The thought of one of us slipping in the racing water and torrential rain with the children, or possibly dropping one, was unbearable. We felt secure in the van and hoped that, at worst, we would have to dry off and somehow eventually get home.

Melissa continued to drive slowly and cautiously through the water, trying to stay in the "tracks" of the vehicle in front of us. Other vehicles were still getting through and even passing us on the left. One of them, a semi tractor-trailer, actually passed us on the left shoulder, right up against the concrete median.

"What? What's he doing?" Melissa shrieked. "He's going to hit us!" He passed us only inches from Melissa's door.

I felt cold water against my feet.

"It's seeping in!" I blurted.

"Oh no!" Melissa gasped.

The situation deteriorated by the second. The water was soaking our feet and everything on the floor. I tried to pick up some belongings, such as our wedding clothes and Melissa's purse, and hang them from the coat hangers. We were still thinking we were going to make it through the water and be okay on the other side once we dried off. The semi, for one, was still making it through.

"Let's stay behind him now," Melissa said.

Ironically, Melissa's brother, Matt, had driven past milepost 116 only two or three minutes before us. He tried to call us but didn't have our cell phone number. So he called their father, Jere, at 8:54 P.M. to try to warn us of the water. Then he called 911. He reported that they couldn't tell there was even water on the highway until they were in the middle of it. He said that the water was splashing on their headlights, and their van had lifted up and come down several times in the water. When his wife asked if they should stop and get out, Matt indicated "No," since they, too, had four small children and couldn't maneuver their van to the right or go in reverse at that point. They made the decision to keep going. They passed someone in the left lane and kept driving through the water. Thankfully, they made it through.

After talking to Matt, Jere immediately tried to call us at 8:57 P.M. Unfortunately, that was the moment we reached Jacob Creek at milepost 116 and splashed into the water. Most of the time, Jacob Creek is a tranquil prairie waterway carrying little more than a trickle and passing innocuously under the Kansas Turnpike. But at that moment it was the center of a torrent later estimated to be 1,000 feet wide.

Our children started waking up. The jittery movements of the van, the commotion, and the worried sounds of our voices interrupted their sleep. Makenah was the first child to wake up, because the rapidly rising water reached her long legs first. Her feet and her belongings were getting wet. She started crying. "Mommy, Daddy— what's happening?" she asked. "My feet are wet! All my stuff is getting wet."

"Don't worry, Makenah," I said as reassuringly as possible. "We're going to be all right. God will protect us."

Alenah heard Makenah and started crying as she awakened. Nicholas soon was crying and whimpering too. At 9:06 P.M., Melissa called her father and spoke for about five minutes while I tended to our children. She explained the situation to him as best she could.

"What do we do? What do we do?" Melissa asked, becoming half-hysterical.

Given the movement and proximity of the semi in front of us, and considering the obvious risks and dangers of trying to get out of the van and navigate through the rising waters on foot, Melissa's father and stepmom agreed that it was safest for us to stay in the van and keep driving. The risks inside appeared less than the risks outside. We said good-bye to Jere and Judy.

The semi that had passed us now stopped in front of us. Melissa was furious. "What's he doing?" she shouted. "Why won't he move? If he would just move forward a little, we could get out of this."

We suspected that we were at the lowest point on the highway, because the road appeared to ascend slightly from the dip we were in. If we could drive forward just 50 yards or so, we could make it out of the dangerous water.

But we couldn't move at all. We were blocked in the front by the semi; in the back by other cars; to the left by the concrete median; and to the right by debris, vehicles that were now floating, and the rising floodwaters. We were trapped.

"It's not stopping, Robert," Melissa said fearfully. "The water's still coming in."

The water had reached the seat cushions when the engine stalled.

"Oh, God!" she screamed. "The engine's dead!"

In fractured sentences, I said, "Roll down the windows a few inches. Give me the keys, but keep the lights on."

We left the running lights and hazard signals on and cracked the driver's side window a few inches—just in case. The electric windows were still working intermittently. I took the keys out of the ignition; they were attached to a long key ring, and I slipped it over my head and around my neck. As I patted my own pockets, I realized that my college graduation watch and my own set of keys had already slipped out of my shorts pocket and were lost somewhere on the floor in the water.

A man came up to my window on the passenger side and knocked hard. I found out later that his name was Ryan Lane. All I could hear from him was muffled yells. I couldn't understand a thing he was trying to say due to the pounding rain and our crying children. I pushed the button to roll down the window, but it wasn't working.

I could hardly see him through the downpour and the darkness. The force of the water prevented my opening the door, and neither Melissa nor I felt right about trying to get out of the van and make our way on foot through the now, waist-high rushing water with four small children—even with the help of a third adult. The man soon left.

If a momentary opportunity of escape ever did exist through the flash flood, it passed before we ever realized just how high the water could rise. Every inch it rose, it seemed it couldn't possibly get any worse. Now there was absolutely no chance we could all safely swim through this raging river with our children. We were truly in God's hands and at His mercy.

By this time, Makenah, Nicholas, and Alenah were all noticeably scared and crying. Zachary was the only one not crying. Because of his Down syndrome, he was probably not quite sure what to make of the situation. In her distress, Makenah got out of her seat belt and came up to stand between us, just behind the front seats.

"Okay, you guys. Let's sing a song together," I said, hoping to shift their thoughts to something familiar and comforting. We chose a song that we had sung many times around the piano at home: "Lord, I Lift Your Name on High."

I recited portions of Psalm 46, saying, "God is my strength; God is my refuge, an ever-present help in time of trouble." We prayed in short, interrupted phrases. Despite the fear and stress of the situation, I sensed an amazing reassuring peace that somehow we were all going to be okay through this. Surely God hadn't seen us through so many trials and difficulties in life to fail us now.

The water was *still* rising. At this point, it was nearly five feet high over the highway and flowing over the concrete median like a waterfall. The rain pounded on the minivan's roof so loudly that it sounded as if we were caught in a hailstorm. Our children wailed with fear. We hoped this was the worst it would get, since the water seemingly couldn't get any higher. The rushing current had pressed our van firmly against the median.

Okay. We can do this, I thought. *With God's help, we can make it through this unthinkable situation.*

Inside the van, the water had now risen to the steering wheel. Our children's heads were still safely above the water level, but the water was bitterly cold. We hoped we could sit this out until the water subsided and then worry about drying off and getting the van towed later.

Amazingly, a man appeared at Melissa's window on the driver's side to try to help.

"Can you help us?" Melissa pleaded. "What's your name?"

He told her it was Al.

"How are you holding on?" Melissa yelled. "Is there any possible way we can get out on foot?"

I couldn't hear what Al was saying to her over the cries of our children. Shouting to be heard, Melissa asked Al if there was any way to form a rope chain to safety. Unfortunately, we only had bungee cords in the van. I was looking back, trying to calm the children, when I heard Melissa holler, "Al! Al!!"

"What happened?" I asked her.

"I thought I saw Al slip in the water!"

We both looked out the window for him, but we couldn't see him anymore. At 9:13 P.M., Melissa tried to call our church for prayer. Through many of the trials we had faced over the past six years, our church congregation had always been a source of support.

"No one's answering this late on a Saturday," she said.

Next, she called Debbie, a friend from church.

"Please pray for us," Melissa pleaded. Then she tried to explain where we were and what was happening. But she wasn't making any sense. Debbie suggested we get on the roof, not realizing why that wasn't possible. She had no way of knowing we were in a swiftly flowing river, not just a pool of water. During the call, Melissa grew more hysterical as the children continued crying.

"We're going to die!" she shouted. "Jesus, save us! Jesus, save us! Jesus, save us!"

Each time the water rose, we kept thinking, *Surely this will end. Surely it can't get any worse.*

It got worse than any of us could have ever imagined.

Suddenly, around 9:18 P.M., everything broke loose. Eyewitnesses from cars that were trapped near the water's edge described a wall of water seven feet high rushing across the freeway. U.S. Geological Survey measurements later estimated that 32,000 gallons of water were racing by each second—the equivalent of a swimming pool full of water five feet deep, 20 feet wide, and 43 feet long.

The force of the water swept 11 sections of the concrete median off the road. Each section was 20 feet long and weighed more than

10,000 pounds. It scattered the concrete barriers down the embankment and beyond into the creek bed. These were the only things
holding our van in place. Once the medians were gone, nothing
remained to protect us from the current.

The wave hit us while Melissa was still talking on the cell phone.
We couldn't see the wall of water coming, but we felt the back of the
van lift up. We seemed to take a nosedive across the two southbound
lanes of traffic and down the embankment. Melissa and our children
screamed as loud as they could. We seemed to hit something, perhaps the culvert, as we crashed with a sudden jolt. It felt as though
we were caught in a powerful waterfall.

We had only moments to save ourselves. Melissa was still on the
phone with Debbie, who could clearly hear everything but was
unclear about what was actually happening. She couldn't envision
the situation from Melissa's short, hysterical phrases.

"We've got to kick out the window!" I said. "We've got to get
everyone out!"

Melissa and I agreed that our only possible means of escape now
was through the driver's side window, in the direction of the raging
torrent. Since I still had my sneakers on, and Melissa had slipped her
sandals off, we switched places so I could kick out the window.
Because I was the stronger swimmer, we agreed I would have the best
chance of rescuing our family.

When I kicked out the window, it was like popping a balloon. I
was instantly sucked out of the van. Our friend Debbie heard the
screams and the part about kicking out the window. After that, her
phone went silent.

I lost all sense of orientation as I was pulled downstream under-
water. It's entirely possible that the van was rolling upside down as
the floodwaters swept it along. I'm convinced that Melissa and

Makenah, who were both out of their seat belts and right next to me, were sucked out immediately behind me. In the urgency, chaos, and confusion, Melissa and I shared no final kiss or words of good-bye with each other or our children.

~

I was drowning.

I could feel myself being tossed up, down, left, and right—like a rag doll tumbling in a washing machine. I had absolutely no control over my movements. I couldn't see or breathe.

I was completely at the mercy of the current—or rather, at the mercy of God.

This can't be the end, I thought. *Not now. Not like this. Our family is just now blossoming so beautifully. It's much too soon.*

Somehow, I wasn't afraid. I felt a tangible, comforting peace of God. I was ingesting water and remember thinking that although I was truly drowning—and sensed my wife and children were as well—our whole family was going to heaven together, and it really wasn't so bad. It was like being in a dream, only this was real. It seemed supernatural. It felt as if God had reached down His hand and cupped our entire family into His palm to personally escort us directly to heaven together.

I felt as if I were "breathing" water—similar to a child inhaling fluid in the womb. Water seemed to flow effortlessly in and out of my lungs—yet it wasn't painful in any way. I still had the key ring around my neck. Amazingly, it didn't catch on a tree branch or a barbed wire fence and strangle me, although it easily could have. Weeds, roots, and branches brushed by my fingertips as I grasped in vain for something—anything—to slow me down.

About a half-mile from the highway, my head lifted above the water. I coughed, gasped for air, and bobbed up and down as I struggled against the torrent. I gulped mouthfuls of water and sank under several more times. The force of the water was unfathomable. Melissa and I had been caught in a riptide in Mexico and rafted in class-4 rapids before. This was much, much worse. Nothing seemed to work as I struggled to survive. I felt myself sinking into the deep again. I could see the shore off to one side, but I couldn't get there.

And then, somehow, by the grace and mercy of God, I found myself near the south bank of Jacob Creek. I grabbed on to something and crawled out of the water on my hands and knees. I was utterly exhausted, in shock, and freezing cold. I called out several times, "Melissa! Melissa!" but I couldn't see or hear anything—not her, not any of our children, not even the van. I could only hear the roar of the water and see sporadic whitecaps atop the rapids. The rain was still pounding down, and the noise was deafening. My feeble attempts to call out to my family felt horribly inadequate.

On my knees, I raised my arms up to heaven and cried out "Oh, God!" over and over. "Oh, God!"

When I tried to stand, my legs buckled under me and I collapsed. My legs felt like jelly. I rose, stumbled a few feet, and fell again.

Time after time, I got up, staggered a few feet, and fell. Soon, my stomach tightened, and I sensed that unmistakable feeling before you get sick. I knelt on the ground and vomited everything I had ingested.

I could see the flashing lights of emergency vehicles on the highway, and I knew I had to go for help if there was any chance of finding and rescuing my family. I crawled toward them as quickly as my body would allow. The rain was still pounding down, and the terrain was rocky and slippery.

About 30 yards from the highway, I climbed over a four-foot barbed wire fence. Because of my exhaustion, it took me about three tries to scale it. I ached to call out for help to people up on the highway, but I was in such shock, so out of breath, and panting so hard that I felt as if I had lost my voice. I finally made my way up the embankment and back onto the highway. By now, nearly an hour had passed since we were swept off the turnpike.

I approached a highway patrol trooper and blurted, "My wife and four children are still down there!"

The patrol car near him was already full, so he escorted me to a kind husband and wife who were both nurses. They had me sit in the backseat of their car and gave me a blanket to keep warm. They suggested I take off my wet shirt to prevent hypothermia and help me warm up. I was in shock, soaking wet, muddy, and colder than I had ever felt in my life.

Soon, I was taken to an ambulance that had arrived on the scene. I remained in the ambulance for three agonizing hours—freezing cold, shivering, and, ironically, incredibly thirsty. But the ambulance had no drinking water. The two gentlemen inside the ambulance were very kind. From time to time, they offered a few words of comfort. Otherwise, the only sounds were the incessant rain outside and the repetitious rhythms of the vital sign monitors hooked to me—compressing and contracting over and over.

It all felt so surreal and utterly unfathomable. I lay there on the cold, hard gurney, wondering where my family was, wondering if the rescue workers had found any of them, wishing I could jump out and look for them myself, wondering if every strange noise I heard outside the ambulance could be them, hoping—praying the ambulance doors would somehow swing open to display the relieved faces of my five family members, safe and sound, glad to see their daddy and husband again. I longed for those words I heard so many times when I came home from work and we were all safe and sound: *"Daddy's home!"*

It never happened.

After the floodwaters over the highway receded enough to drive through, and the authorities were sure there weren't any more immediate survivors, I was taken by ambulance north to Newman Memorial Hospital in Emporia. It was 1:10 A.M., nearly four hours after the wall of water hit us.

The highway patrol trooper said it was a miracle I was alive.

A miracle, indeed.

3

Where Is My Family?

The trip to the hospital in Emporia covered only 11 miles, but it seemed to take forever. My shock and disbelief on that bumpy ride were compounded by the disorientation of riding backward while lying on my back on a hard surface.

This can't be happening, I kept saying to myself.

Not to me. Not to us. Not my beautiful family, who only hours before had bounced around at a wedding reception and an ice cream store. But now they were gone—out of my reach.

By the time we reached the hospital, it was nearly 1:30 A.M. They wheeled me on the gurney from the ambulance into the emergency room. Several nurses tended to the cuts on my right leg. They removed the thick blanket that had covered me in the ambulance, and the cold hospital air hit my body as if I'd entered a walk-in freezer. I flashed back to the frigid waters I had churned in just hours earlier, when I was so close to death.

I still had on my wet shorts, shoes, and socks. The key ring clung to my neck.

The nurse took the wet, wadded-up shirt at my side and the key ring and handed me a thin hospital gown to cover my upper body.

They helped me down off the gurney and into a wheelchair to take me to the X-ray room. As they wheeled me down the hallway, the cold air flowing against my arms and chest through the hospital gown felt like a frigid fan blowing directly on me. I shivered almost uncontrollably with a tightness and cringing pain in the pit of my stomach. My mouth and body were parched from dehydration and shock. I hadn't yet had anything to drink.

The nurse slowly wheeled me into the X-ray room and shot several angles of my lungs as I stood against a wall in various positions. After she finished, I asked for a drink. She wheeled me down the hallway once again with the chilly air pressing against my stomach and chest, and I finally got a sip of water. It felt so good to have some sort of sustenance enter my body.

The doctor came and checked me from head to toe and examined the X-rays. Miraculously, all looked well. There was no lung damage, only cuts, scrapes, and bruises. A nurse came into the emergency room and said that Melissa's father, Jere, was on the phone. He was calling from a Kansas Turnpike Authority station only a few miles away.

This would be the hardest moment of my life to that point. Jere was frantic, asking how I was and what had happened. When he last spoke to us on the cell phone, water was pouring into the van, rising to the seat cushions, and stalling the engine. After we had ended our call, he had called his son Matt and his family and decided to meet them in Topeka.

They agreed that their wives and Matt's four children should proceed the two hours home in their van to Hiawatha in northeast Kansas. Jere and Matt drove back in the car to the Kansas Turnpike Authority station in Emporia and waited while a dispatcher tried to find us.

"I'm okay, Jere," I said, my voice trembling. "But they can't find Melissa and our kids. I'm so sorry."

"What!?" he shrieked. "What!? What!? Oh no! Oh no! No!"

I felt so empty and helpless telling Melissa's father that she could not be found. Jere said that he and Matt would come right away.

I knew another terrible phone call awaited me: to my parents in Cincinnati. The nurse showed me how to dial out. It was almost 3:00 A.M. at my parents' home. My fingers shook as I struggled to remember their number and experienced one of my first real feelings of being completely alone in this world.

Over the course of our 13 and a half years together, Melissa and I had developed a rhythm and flow to our relationship. We knew each other's strengths and weaknesses and compensated for each other. Melissa was great with phone numbers, not me. I eventually managed to remember the area code and number and placed the receiver by my ear. One ring. Two rings. *Please pick up,* I pleaded mentally. Three rings, and still no answer. Both of my hands were now shaking.

Because he had arthritis, my father was usually a light sleeper. To help him sleep, my parents often turned down the volume on the phone at night. The answering machine clicked on.

Oh no, I thought. *What do I do? This is not the sort of message you leave on an answering machine.*

And yet I knew I must tell them what had happened. They would want to know immediately. I didn't know when I would have another chance to call them.

"Mom and Dad, this is Robert," I said, my voice calm. "I'm okay, but we were caught in a flash flood in Kansas coming home from Wichita and, well . . . they can't find Melissa or any of our children. I don't know where they are!"

My control melted, and I was weeping as I continued.

"I'm at a hospital in Emporia, Kansas. Please call me at this number. I love you guys. Good-bye."

I felt utterly alone, empty, and stripped of all that I was. All that was valuable to me was missing. Nothing on this earth seemed to matter any longer. The hospital staff treated the cuts on my legs and arms, and then I was discharged.

But to what? Where was my family? Where would I go? I signed the hospital forms with shaking hands and tried in vain to pay attention to the kind nurse's instructions. She offered me some medication to help me relax, if I needed it. I had been in hospitals so many times before: for the births of our first three children, for Melissa's third arthroscopic knee surgery, for her emergency surgery following a miscarriage. I had been there for so many operations, treatments, clinics, and therapies for Zachary's Down syndrome complications; and for Alenah's cardiology clinic to check her pulmonary stenosis, a heart valve condition, shortly after we returned from China.

Only once had I ever been the patient—and that was for a routine checkup procedure without complications. I was always the one who was well, the one in control, the one who provided for our family. I was always the one who pulled out the insurance card, signed the papers, bought the medication, and paid the deductibles or co-pays.

But everything was upside down now. This time, I was the patient. I had no family by my side, no wallet, credit cards, or insurance cards. I had only my saturated clothes and the key ring from the van.

I found myself thinking the same thing over and over: *This can't possibly be happening.*

The thoughtful staff at Newman Memorial Hospital took me

upstairs to an unused wing, even though I had been discharged. I was still shaky, so they took me there in a wheelchair. They allowed me to stay as a "guest" in an empty room. I changed into a hospital gown and crawled under the covers to try to warm up.

"Can I bring you some more blankets?" the nurse asked.

"Yes, please," I managed to mutter.

The nurse brought in several thick blankets, which must have been warmed in some sort of oven. I could feel the weight of them on my body, but nothing seemed to penetrate the cold permeating me. Even though I had survived the flood with only minor injuries, it felt as if something had been ripped out of me.

She turned out every light except the one in the bathroom. She left the bathroom door slightly ajar, and a ray of light fell onto the tile floor of my room. I was under so many blankets, and yet it felt as if I were shivering to death. I just couldn't get warm.

I took one of the tiny pills the nurse had provided to help me relax, but it did about as much good as the concrete medians against the force of the flash flood. I tried to close my eyes, but sleep just wasn't possible. After the darkness of the night, the darkness in the water, and the darkness I felt engulfing my heart, I found I wanted to keep my eyes open. So I locked onto the ray of light beaming across the room as I slipped into a daze.

Sometime around 3:00 A.M., Jere and Matt found the hospital and were led by a nurse to my room. I could faintly hear their uneasy voices down the hallway as they approached. I slowly slipped out from under the covers to meet them. They walked into my room with a look of shock and grief on their faces. No words were spoken. None could ever have been adequate. The three of us immediately embraced and wept.

I tried to explain what had happened. They shook their heads as

I went through the details. I can only imagine that Matt was picturing himself in my shoes, since he had come so close to being stranded in the water in his minivan with his family just a few minutes before us. We speculated about what could have happened to Melissa and our children. Matt made some mention that while he and Jere were at the turnpike authority trying to find us, they thought they had heard on the police radio that our van had been found upright. Perhaps my family was okay? We were pondering every possible scenario, even miraculous ones.

Jere left the room to call his wife, Judy, and relay my condition and more of the details. Still shivering, I crawled back under the blankets to try to warm up. Matt sat in the chair next to the bed.

I sank into a steady daze, staring at the ceiling, listening to Matt praying aloud by my side. I was still in shock, and my body was still trembling, but even so, as I lay there, I began feeling something deep within—a supernatural peace that could only have come from God, because my mind and heart were grappling with what had just happened to my family and me.

Back in Kansas City, Debbie—the friend who had been talking to Melissa when the wall of water hit our van—called our pastor after her phone went silent and told him what she knew. Pastor Jerls had called the local FOX TV affiliate to try to get more information. They also called the Kansas Turnpike Authority at 10:00 P.M., recounting the details of Debbie's final conversation with Melissa and giving them the names of our family members to help in the search. Debbie and Pastor Jerls decided to drive through the dark, dangerous weather to help out in any way possible.

I later learned that many Kansas agencies, departments, and private citizens mobilized in the middle of the night to look for my family and for Al Larson, who had also been swept away. They scoured the land on foot and with four-wheelers. They even tried to navigate the raging river in the darkness of night with a small boat, but the current was just too treacherous. They asked for helicopters, but the wind and weather were too severe. Over the next several days, many individuals spent hour after hour away from their families, trying to find mine.

A rescue worker and a fireman from Emporia came across our van at 2:59 A.M., which was about the same time Jere and Matt reached my hospital room. The van was upside down a mile and a half from the highway. The water had been so deep and powerful that our van had completely cleared a four-foot barbed wire fence about a mile from the highway. The force of the water had been so strong that the van was crushed beyond recognition: The windshield and windows were blown out, the tailgate was mangled and hanging open, all the doors were dented and jammed into place, and the roof was compacted as if a monster had stepped on it like a toy.

The rescue worker was a kind and gentle father himself. He later told me that he knew the conditions were tragically bad when they approached my van for the first time. I can only imagine how ghastly the scene was for them: searching with flashlights in the rain and darkness, then finding the children still strapped in their safety seats.

The rescue worker and the fireman had to work through the sliding-door window, prying back portions of the door, just to cut the seat belts off the car seats and free my lifeless children. Nicholas was closest to the sliding door in the middle row, so the fireman freed him first. He gently handed him to the rescue worker, who laid his small body on the shore. Next, the fireman reached for Zachary in the backseat, freed him, and gently passed him over as well.

The conditions were extremely dangerous for the rescue workers. Rain was still pounding down, and the raging river was still shifting the van. The fireman couldn't easily reach Alenah. She was in her car seat against the window on the far side of the van. But he didn't give up on her, and before long she was lying next to her two older brothers.

There was no sign of Makenah or Melissa.

The rescue worker, whom I had never met before, said that when he saw my three children lying there on the shore next to each other, he could tell that they were loved. The way they looked, how they were dressed, how Alenah's hair was fixed. . . . He told me he sensed that they had a sweet, sweet spirit about them. Amid all the horrifying and perilous conditions that night, he noticed, somehow, that the presence of the Lord was truly there.

As they were retrieving our children from the van, I was lying in bed, listening to Matt pray at my side.

Jere paced the hallway, crying with even deeper desperation with each phone call to his wife. I remained severely disoriented—much as I had felt in the water as I was being tossed like a rag doll. It seemed as though I had suddenly lost my compass . . . my true north . . . my identity. How fitting that my wallet and my license— my identification—were gone, along with all the pictures of my family that I carried in my wallet. In an instant, everything I was— father, provider, protector—had been washed away.

I kept reliving the chaotic events of those final 20 minutes in the van. *Why couldn't I protect my family? How could this have happened? How could God let this happen to us? Did Melissa and our children watch me get sucked out? Did they have a chance? Did they suffer? Did they drown? Did they survive? How did I wind up on the bank of the river? Oh, God! How could You let this happen? How? Why, God? Why? Why us?*

4

"They're with Jesus Now"

I heard the footsteps shortly after 5:00 A.M.

They were slow and heavy, made by leather boots, and they were heading toward my room.

No, please don't do this, I thought.

An officer and a chaplain entered my room, their hats on their chests. I knew what was coming. I was shaking, dreading their next words with every fiber of my body.

"Mr. Rogers," the officer began hesitantly, "we found your van . . . and we have the awkward task of having to ask you to identify the bodies of your three youngest children."

I felt the blood drain from my head.

My mind raced. *What? All three? My little Zachary, Nicholas, and Alenah? What?! What about Makenah and Melissa? Where are they?*

His words pierced me like a dagger, driving clear through my heart. I have no idea what I said to them at that moment. What words would have been useful? This was unbearable. And yet, it confirmed what I had already sensed in my heart. They were with Jesus. They were fine. In an instant, it was horrible and beautiful at the same time.

A sudden calm, a palpable peace, wrapped around me like a blanket and filled me. It was like receiving a hearty hug from a life-long friend at just the right time. I felt a strength, a courage, and a resolve that I would not have been able to muster myself. For years, I had heard the words of Jesus in church—"Peace I leave with you; my peace I give you" (John 14:27). I had learned that the Holy Spirit is actually called the "Comforter" and that He is the "God of all comfort, who comforts us in all our troubles" (2 Corinthians 1:3–4). These words were very real to me because our family embraced a lifestyle of a real relationship with God as a Father and as a Friend.

From all the years of crying out to Him in the midst of our deepest pain—during childbirth, during Zachary's surgeries, during Down syndrome complications, during Alenah's adoption, during marital disagreements, during months of more bills than pay-checks—during all sorts of trials—we turned *to* God rather than *away* from God. In those times of deepest pain, we grew to know and receive God's deepest presence. When we trusted Him during those times that didn't make sense, God revealed His deepest and most intimate loving nature.

Sometimes it manifested itself in the form of a warmth within us or as a soft whisper of assurance in our hearts. Sometimes we felt Him in a little miraculous moment—a strange turn of events—that we knew only God could have arranged. However it showed itself, we knew the source was God and the result was His peace. We trusted Him, and He blessed us in the midst of brokenness.

At the hospital in Emporia, He showed Himself in the amazing peace that filled me as I absorbed the words I dreaded most. It didn't cause the pain or the tragedy to go away. It didn't transport me away from it even for a moment. I could not escape the horrific reality. Rather, God's peace and strength met me right where I was, right when I needed it, right as my world was falling apart. It made the moment bearable. That could only be the gift of God's generous grace.

So many times on my way to work over the years, I had prayed Psalm 112. Now those words came back to me:

> Even in darkness light dawns for the upright, for the gracious and compassionate and righteous man. . . . Surely he will never be shaken; a righteous man will be remembered forever. He will have no fear of bad news; his heart is steadfast, trusting in the LORD. His heart is secure, he will have no fear. (verses 6–8)

With God's strength, not my own, I could face what I was being asked to do.

"Okay," I said. "Let's go."

Matt and Jere were in shock and disbelief, crying profusely.

"Jere, are you up to coming with me?" I asked.

He shook his head no.

"Matt, can you come with me?"

Matt hesitated, and then he reluctantly agreed. He was Melissa's brother, yet he felt like my brother, too. They led us down that third-floor hallway to an employee elevator. No words were spoken, except for an occasional "This way, Mr. Rogers." My head somberly drifted down, my eyes watching the ground and glancing ahead only when absolutely necessary. I felt like someone emerging from a dark movie theater into the daylight, blinded by bright sunlight. It was as if I were trying to shield my eyes from the pain I knew was imminent.

We got off the elevator on the first floor, turned left, and walked down a short hallway to a set of double doors. Someone pushed a button on the wall, and the doors slowly opened. It felt as if my entire life were flashing before my eyes. It seemed as if everyone was moving in slow motion.

This had to be a movie. This had to be happening to someone else—not me. But I was the one everyone was staring at. ER nurses at the nurses station and in the hallway froze in their tracks as they spotted me and realized what was about to occur. That hallway seemed to go on forever. I was so nervous that all I could do was focus on putting one foot in front of the other. We finally came to a stop in the large emergency room where I was treated just hours before.

The room was dark now. Different. A curtain covered the entrance. I recognized that muddy, cold, rainwater stench that I had inhaled when I crawled out of Jacob Creek on my hands and knees nearly eight hours earlier.

They drew back the curtain.

Time stopped.

There before me was my life: flesh of my flesh, bone of my bone, heart of my heart. My two sons and daughter. Zachary—my little big guy. Nicholas—my buddy boy. Alenah—my sweet pea.

Desperation, horror, agony, and anguish washed through me at that moment. I felt utterly paralyzed. A pain in the pit of my stomach welled up within me, and I groaned deeply—syllables I had never pronounced and could never repeat. I wanted to be on the table next to them.

I gravitated to my first son, Zachary. I collapsed across his chest. "Oh, Zachary! Oh, my sweet, sweet Zachary!"

I sobbed like a baby. He didn't smell like the sweet Zachary I knew—so fair in his complexion, hair, and soft skin. He smelled like the raging water from the night before. It was awful. This was my son! How could this be? I somehow mustered the energy to lift my head and look at his face, my cheeks now drenched with tears and cold from pressing against his chest.

Zachary looked . . . angelic . . . peaceful . . . whole . . . at rest. He wasn't all bruised as I would have expected. It was surprising, especially considering the pictures I saw of our van in the newspaper later that week. He looked completely fine. This was my son who had brought forth in me greater faith and trust in the Almighty— first through his conception and then through the endless challenges of Down syndrome. Before our very eyes, we had seen God turn what we thought was a tragedy into a triumph. Through him, I had learned so much about persistence and never giving up.

Now he was free indeed. He would have no disability in heaven. I whispered into his ear, "Be healed, Zachary." I lifted my head, stood up straight, placed my hands on his body, and recalled the words of Jesus on the cross. Paraphrasing Luke 23:46, I said, "Father, into Your hands I commend his spirit."

The words of that song we sang many times, "Jesus Loves Me," became painfully ironic: "Little ones to Him belong." My children never fully belonged to me. They belonged to Him. They were a gift from God. Now they were back in His presence.

At that moment, the concept of heaven and eternity was more real to me than ever before. I placed my hand on Zachary's forehead, just as I had done in the van hours before, and I stumbled through the same blessing, one last time, choking on the words:

"May the Lord bless you, heal you, keep you, and protect you. May He make His face shine upon you and give you peace and favor all the days of your life. In Jesus' name, Amen."

As I kissed his forehead, I kissed death. Yet, amazingly, it had no victory over me or Zachary. My grief still tore at me, but death had lost its sting because I knew through Christ it represented our passage into eternal life. I was convinced that the glory of God's face was now shining upon Zachary in heaven. In the midst of that horrible moment, I could feel the glory through the agony.

As I stood up, I could hear Matt crying out to God as he wept over his niece and nephews. "God, what are You doing? What are You doing?"

I moved over to Nicholas, my second son . . . my kind, adventurous buddy boy. I cried and kissed and caressed him as I had Zachary. Nicholas, too, looked perfect and angelic. Not even a scratch that I could see.

"Be healed, Nicholas," I said.

As much as I wanted him with me, I couldn't hold him back from the whole new world he was now exploring. I couldn't help but think of the immense awe and wonderment Nicholas had displayed for the simple things on earth. "Hey, Dad, look! It's an airplane!" I tried to imagine how he wondered at heaven's marvels. Only, I desperately wanted his smile and enthusiasm here with me.

I placed my hand on his forehead and blessed Nicholas one last time. Then, as I did with Zachary, I placed my hands on his chest, stood upright, leaned my head back, and said, "Father, into Your hands I commend his spirit."

As I approached my little sweet pea, Alenah, I could think only of how I wanted to keep her all to myself for the rest of her life. I knew she was in heaven, yet my heart was longing for her smile, her warmth, her budding vocabulary, and the way she was just starting to say "Da-da." We had poured so much of our hearts and lives into getting her here from China. She was worth it all. But now my heart felt shattered.

Oh, why did it all have to end like this, less than a year later? Why, God?

"Be healed, Alenah," I whispered into her ear. I knew she wouldn't have a heart defect in heaven. I kissed her, blessed her, and released her to heaven as I had my two sons.

Just the day before, they had each displayed such energy, joy, and exuberance. Now, their lifeless bodies lay on tables in a hospital. It didn't seem real.

I had done what they'd asked me to do: I had identified the bodies of three of my children. Could life get any worse than this? What would I tell Makenah? How would I even begin to approach Melissa? Were they still alive?

The officer and chaplain escorted me back to my room on the third floor. I crawled into the bed and under the now-cold blankets. I was stunned. For now, I couldn't cry. All I could do was stare into the darkness of my cold room.

At the very time I was identifying my three youngest children, my parents were awakening in Cincinnati for Sunday morning church. Dad gradually migrated out of bed, fighting the daily stiffness in his joints from a virtual lifetime of battling arthritis, compounded with multiple foot surgeries and two total knee replacements. He crossed from the upstairs bedroom to the loft where the answering machine sat on the office desk.

He noticed a new message on the machine that must have come after they went to bed the night before. Dad knelt down on one knee and pressed the Play button. For my father, who had prayed diligently for over five decades for the safety of his eight children and numerous grandchildren, what he heard next was a nightmare. He listened to me relate where I was and what had happened. He yelled across the house to my mother because he couldn't believe what he was hearing.

"Francie!"

I can't imagine the anguish that must have flooded my parents' hearts. They played the message over and over and struggled to make sense of the few fragments of description I gave them. They wrote down the phone number and called the hospital in Emporia. I was in my room when the call came through. A kind nurse brought me a cordless phone.

"Mr. Rogers. It's your mother and father," she said.

Thank God, I thought, knowing how they have always been able to bring comfort in the midst of turmoil.

I rolled over on my side in the bed and placed the phone to my ear.

"Hi, Mom and Dad . . . Not so good. . . . I love you, too. Um . . . they found Zachary, Nicholas, and Alenah in our van. They're with Jesus now. I just had to identify them."

My throat constricted as if someone were choking me. I couldn't believe the words that were coming out of my mouth. As best I could, I went on to tell them how it happened. Dad was vigilantly praying, even during the call.

"I love you, Mom and Dad. . . . Okay . . . I'll see you whenever you can get here."

Mom and Dad hung up the phone and burst into tears. They lined up a flight to Kansas City, then they called my oldest sibling, Paul, to give him the news. As the oldest, Paul took on the responsibility of notifying the rest of the family.

Back at the hospital in Emporia, one of the nurses told me my children would be taken to Topeka for an autopsy, and she gave me the chance to see them one last time before they went. I couldn't pass up the opportunity to see and touch my children again, though it was just as difficult the second time.

Ten miles away in the Flint Hills of Kansas, dawn was breaking. Rescue crews scoured the area for Melissa and Makenah. The floodwaters were receding, and at 7:47 A.M., the search for Makenah ended. She was perhaps a quarter mile from the van, up against a barbed wire fence.

About three hours later, an officer came to my room and said, "Mr. Rogers, we found Makenah."

While I knew in my heart that those words were inevitable, I still fought them.

No, I thought. *Not my sweet, dainty Makenah, too. Not my peanut butter cup. Not Daddy's first little girl. Not my last remaining child.*

All four of my precious children . . . dead.

How cruel that seemed, given all we had endured to bring them into this world. I had inwardly hoped that Makenah was light enough to bob to the surface as I had and somehow grab on to a tree or swim to shore. She had taken swimming lessons since infancy. If anyone was light enough and strong enough to swim and survive, I had thought it might be Makenah. And yet I couldn't imagine explaining to her that her two brothers and new sister from China were dead. How would I explain that the good and loving God we constantly spoke of since her birth could permit this to happen to her family?

As painful as it was to know that Makenah was gone, I still had the comfort of knowing that all four of my children were with Jesus, with His loving arms wrapped around them. If it weren't for that glimmer of hope, the pain would have been unbearable.

They slowly led me again to the first floor and down that long hallway. We turned right, into a small examination room. They opened the door, and I walked in with Pastor Jerls, Matt, and one or two others. I scarcely noticed any of the other people or surroundings. It was only Makenah and me . . . my firstborn daughter and her daddy. Since Melissa was unable to hold Makenah at first due to her C-section and ensuing recovery, I was the first one to cuddle her and sing a lullaby to her. I was the one who announced her name immediately after the two doctors lifted her into this world.

Now as I gazed upon her in that hospital room in Emporia, Kansas, Makenah's life was complete. Just as I had been the first one to hold her, now I was the last to embrace her. She had taught me so much about how it felt to be a daddy; she was such a well-behaved little girl and a great first child; she taught me what it was like to be someone's hero. And yet, even as her hero, I wasn't able to save her life.

How would I respond without breaking down when someone asked, "Do you have children?"

How would I explain this to Melissa? So many questions and emotions raced through my mind. My eyes locked onto Makenah. She looked so incredibly peaceful and beautiful—just as she had on so many nights after bedtime when I would peer through her door and gaze in wonderment at God's precious gift to Melissa and me. Now she was with God. I stroked her hair and kissed her forehead. Once again, I had to surrender. I whispered into her ear, "Be healed, Makenah. Dance with Jesus."

As they gently led me back to my room, the reality grew with each step: All four of my children were dead.

Curling up on the hard hospital bed, my thoughts turned again to Melissa and the words she had uttered just eight months earlier in the Kansas City International Airport upon our return from China. Amid all the joy of adopting Alenah, Melissa ached from the separation from our three oldest children.

After two weeks in China, we were the last ones to disembark the plane in Kansas City. We scurried down the Jetway and entered the airport terminal, beaming from ear to ear. Melissa was holding Alenah in her arms. I dropped our bags, and we both ran to embrace our family. The joy and relief we felt—knowing that we were finally all safe and sound, together once again—was overwhelming. My sister Anne had cared for our children during the two-week trip, and Melissa wept as she hugged her.

"I'll never leave them like that again—ever," Melissa whispered into Anne's ear as they held each other that day at the airport.

Less than a year later, all four of our children were gone. What would Melissa do now? How could she possibly bear this? I knew how deeply our two miscarriages had devastated her. What would I say to her now? How would I even begin to break the news? Where was my bride? Was she even alive? Was she wandering aimlessly somewhere? Where could she be? I needed her. I needed to bury my face in her shoulder and just cry.

But now all I could do was bury my face in the sterile hospital pillow and cry without ceasing.

5

Hoping Against Hope

After my solemn, final moment with Makenah, the pace of everything seemed to quicken.

I rarely had a moment to myself just to take a breath and collect my thoughts. Chaos descended as friends and relatives of Melissa's parents began pouring in. They congregated in the hospital's third-floor lobby. Everyone was trying to comprehend this dreadful tragedy.

The staff at Newman Memorial Hospital allowed us to gather by ourselves in the lobby area so we could have some degree of privacy. Staff members started bringing trays and carts of cookies, drinks, and sandwiches—all without charge. There was even a card circulating among the staff for me, expressing their condolences. It was as if everyone felt the need to help in any way they could.

I later learned that the hospital staff also ran "interference" between us and all the media who were calling and trying to find me—the only known survivor—for an interview. When they called to ask, the hospital truthfully responded, "I'm sorry. Mr. Rogers is no longer a patient here." It was true, since I had already been discharged. Still, it was considerate of them to give us a layer of privacy.

Mom and Dad arrived at Kansas City International Airport at about 11:00 A.M., where they found my brother Mark waiting for them at the curbside. They immediately left for Emporia, and Mom called me on their cell phone.

"Robert, dear? How are you?" she asked. "We just got to Kansas City. Mark is driving us to Emporia now. We'll be there as soon and as safely as we can."

"Thanks, Mom," I said, getting out of bed and pacing the cold hospital floor. "I love you guys . . . um, Mom? I just had to identify Makenah. They found her, too. Mom? They're all with Jesus."

I could scarcely force the words out without collapsing from grief. It still just wasn't conceivable that I was talking about my own children all being in heaven already. Mom burst into tears as I heard her share the news with Dad and Mark.

"Oh, Robert . . . we'll be there as soon as we can."

I set the phone down and made my way over toward the bed. A nurse came to my room with several bags of gifts.

"Mr. Rogers? I thought you could use some of these things."

I was amazed at what I saw. A Wal-Mart bag was filled with new shoes, socks, and underwear, and another bag held slightly used clothes.

"These are some clothes that used to fit my husband. You look like you're about the size he once was—that is, before he put on weight."

She succeeded in helping me smile—ever so slightly—for the first time since my family and I enjoyed that ice cream together at Braum's before leaving Wichita. I was humbled and speechless. All of my clothes were either drenched or dirty from the muddy river water. Since my arrival at the hospital, I'd worn only thin, papery hospital gowns.

After finishing her shift, this sympathetic nurse had gone home to pick out some shirts, shorts, and sweats for me; then she went to Wal-Mart and bought a brand-new pair of shoes, a bag of new socks, and a package of new underwear for me. She was still in her hospital work attire, so she must have come back to the hospital just to give them to me. I was amazed and deeply grateful.

"Thank you so much," I said as we embraced. "I don't know what to say."

I was hugging and crying with more visitors in the third-floor lobby shortly after 1:00 P.M. when I caught glimpses of CNN headlines and pictures on the television. They were starting to report on the flash flood, and the caption at the bottom of the screen pierced my heart anew: "Four confirmed dead in Kansas flash flood. Two still missing." Those were *my* four children!

I went out into the hallway to talk to Jere. Out of the corner of my eye, I saw the elevator door open. I found myself hoping that Melissa would come walking out safe and sound. Oh, how I longed for her radiant smile, her cheery step, and her bouncy hair to brighten the gloom that hovered over the room. But it wasn't Melissa; my parents and my brother Mark stepped off the elevator.

I bolted across the room, embraced my parents, and wept. I led them to my room and explained everything I could.

A nurse appeared with the phone in her hand and said, "It's the governor—Governor Sebelius—for you, Mr. Rogers."

I was surprised to receive such a call. The governor expressed her deepest condolences on behalf of the state of Kansas. I accepted them as best I could and mentioned how kind everyone had been.

As the day crawled along, highway patrol troopers came and went, checking on me and giving me the latest information on the search for Melissa. There was still no sign of her. They also started bringing articles from the van that were scattered for more than a mile from the turnpike along the creek bed. Among those items was the camera bag, holding the camera and two rolls of undeveloped film in plastic cylinders. I prayed that they could somehow be salvaged.

The police also handed me scraps of paper with names and numbers from news organizations that were calling for interviews: CNN, *Inside Edition*, AP, NBC's *Today Show*, CBS, and others. They suggested holding a press conference. I knew nothing about how to do that, but they assured me they would handle it.

"We'll set it up at a local hotel for tomorrow morning," I was told. "We'll escort you, your parents, and your pastor there and back. Just read your statement and don't take any questions."

After conferring with my parents, I agreed to the press conference for the next morning: Monday, September 1.

I wanted to call my good friends since college, Janet and Kirk, who lived in Indiana. But I couldn't remember their phone number. Thankfully, I knew our neighbors' number.

Kerry answered the phone, and I told him what happened. Kerry had evidently seen the preliminary local news reports about the flash flood, but he had not yet made the connection to us. All he could say was, "Oh no! Oh no!" I could hear him relay it all to his wife, Mica, in the background, who then started screaming hysterically. Melissa and Mica had become great friends over the past six years, and their friendship flourished as Kerry and Mica adopted a little boy from Korea, and then as we adopted Alenah from China.

After our phone call, Mica took some pink ribbon and scissors and went to our yard, tying pink ribbons around every tree, fence pole, and signpost. Her children followed her around our yard asking all sorts of unanswerable questions. She put candles and flowers in the middle of a grass "island" in our side yard—bordered by the street on one side and our half-circle driveway on the other. She began a neighborhood memorial to our family that quickly grew as news of the tragedy spread.

In the hallway at the hospital, I came upon one of Jere's long-time friends and one of Melissa's spiritual "mentors" growing up—a grand, towering man of faith named Malcolm. Over the years, he and his family had all become trusted friends to Melissa and me. Now, his enormous arms embracing me felt like a refuge from the storm that engulfed me.

I asked him for a favor: to track down a copy of "It Is Well with My Soul," an old hymn written by a man whose four children had drowned in the Atlantic Ocean.

"I just need to reflect on those words for a bit," I told him.

It was nearly 4:00 P.M. when a tall woman dressed in a business suit and carrying a briefcase approached me. I had never met her before. She was kind and gentle, yet clearly out of place among all those in the third-floor lobby who were grieving.

"Hello, Mr. Rogers. I'm with the Midwest Transplant Network. Could I please have a moment with you in private?"

I immediately knew this was about donating my children's organs. Melissa and I had discussed organ donation many times, and we had both checked the box on our driver's licenses to approve organ donation. We knew full well that if anything had ever happened to us or our children, we would gladly donate what organs we could.

As she filled out the forms and continued her litany of questions, I felt as if I were in a trance answering all these details about my own children, as if they were still alive, and we were just going through the general procedures before being admitted to a hospital. It seemed as if Melissa were just downstairs parking the car and would be up any moment. But my children weren't being admitted to a hospital. They were being taken to the coroner's office in Topeka for autopsies.

The opportunity to donate tissues that could save other lives was the first glimmer of hope to pierce through this tragedy. I always knew God promised that He could work all things for the good of those that love Him and are called according to His purpose (Romans 8:28). We had seen it proved time and time again in our lives, and it was happening once more.

Life out of death. That's the message of the gospel. Beauty out of ashes. That's what God promises in chapter 61 of the Book of Isaiah. I was living these scriptures, through flesh of my flesh and bone of my bone. It felt so good to give, but so painful to let go.

In a way, it resembled what Jesus did for us at Calvary. He gave His own life to save ours. I suddenly felt an infinitely deeper closeness and kinship with the fellowship of Jesus' sufferings—and even with God the Father—who gave His only Son, Jesus, to die for us that we might live. I was now signing the papers to surrender my own children in death so that other people's children might live.

I knew I was doing the right thing. I knew I was doing what Melissa would want.

Melissa . . . where was Melissa? How would I ever explain all of this to her? Why couldn't they find her? Oh, how my heart ached to hold the one I called "my love, my life, my friend" on our wedding day and whom I still referred to daily as "my love."

After Elaine, the woman from the transplant network, left, I needed some time alone. I took the elevator downstairs and found the chapel on the first floor. It was empty, quiet, and dimly lit. I sat in a pew and gazed upon a Bible—the book we based our lives on . . . the book I was counting on being the Truth . . . the book we had memorized so much of and relied on for our family's provisions, health, and safety.

I couldn't help but wonder if I had totally missed it. *God, did I mess up somewhere? Did we do something wrong? Did we miss You somehow? Why did You fail us at the hour of our death—the hour we most needed You? What happened, God?*

6

Where the Rubber Meets the Road

Even as I asked those painful questions, I could sense that God was there with me. His peace was tangible amid my questions and fears. After Jesus died and was buried, the apostles were crushed and disheartened by His abrupt absence and by God's silence. Similarly, even though it seemed as though God was absent and silent, He was really the most present He had ever been in my life.

A short time later, Dad spotted me as he spoke with someone on his cell phone, and he motioned for me to follow him. We went toward the end of an empty hallway into a storage room with stacks of hospital beds and fixtures. Dad handed me the phone, and I heard the sweet, comforting, yet crushed voice of my close friend Janet Hughes. Talking with her felt like a warm compress.

I knew that with their young daughter and their business and employees, it would be difficult for Janet and Kirk to just pick up and fly to Kansas City on a moment's notice. But as soon as we got off the phone, Janet and Kirk made the decision to come and be with me during this painful time.

Dennis, my boss of nearly three years, arrived at the hospital later that Sunday afternoon after driving in from Kansas City. He was obviously shaken but still tried to exhibit the upbeat demeanor he displayed so often around the office. He had been through divorce and other life challenges and had figured out how not to remain a victim forever. He knew, and had modeled for me, how to exhibit a positive attitude during trying circumstances.

Dennis knew my analytical nature well enough to know that I would already be blaming myself and reassessing the decisions we were forced to make during the chaos of the previous night. And he was right.

My mind had been dwelling on every decision I had made. I was reliving the events, picking apart every detail. *Did I blow it? Could I have done something more? Was it my fault my children perished? Should I have done something different? Did I do enough? Should I have insisted on driving?*

I kept second-guessing how I had acted and reacted on our final night together as a family. I wrestled with a basic question: Why did I live and they die?

I didn't feel guilty for surviving. But I did feel guilty for not adequately protecting my family. I felt as though I had failed in one of my primary duties as a father; I had failed as a man, as a husband, and as a father.

As an electrical engineer and mathematician himself, Dennis knew the myriad variables that must have lined up for such a catastrophic event to occur—the rate of rain; the timing of the flash flood; the location of the flood; the pace of our van; the length of the wedding reception; the time saying good-bye to relatives, eating at the ice cream parlor, and refueling the van.

Dennis knew that one minor change in a seemingly insignificant event could alter the outcome drastically. He also understood from his own life experiences that it was fruitless to rehash the details and second-guess actions. No amount of rehashing or second-guessing could change the outcome, and it wouldn't accomplish anything.

"Robert, this is no place for should have, would have, or could have," he told me after he arrived. "You absolutely can't beat yourself up over something like this."

His words resonated deeply within me. I recognized that nothing I could think or do now would change history. Nothing could bring back my family. Nothing could change that night's catastrophic outcome. I would have to counter my guilty feelings with uplifting words from Scripture. I would need to remember that what mattered most now was not my actions *from* last night but my reactions *to* last night.

My response to this calamity would set the course for the life I still had left to live. I could spend the rest of my life in pity, feeling sorry for myself, and trying to affix blame. But if I did that, I would only imprison myself. It would serve no good whatsoever. From this moment on, I wanted to do good. I wanted my family's lives to count for something.

I went back to my room to try to have a moment of solitude. The grief and chaos out in the hallway and lobby were becoming too much for me to bear. A short time later, Pastor Jerls came in to check on me. He mentioned a funeral home in our hometown of Liberty that he was familiar with.

"Funeral home?" I said in disbelief.

I didn't want to even consider the notion that all my children would soon be laid out for everyone to mourn at some cold, stale funeral home. But I trusted my pastor's judgment.

"Go ahead, Pastor," I said in surrender. "Please contact them and start making the necessary arrangements for my children's funeral."

"Very well, Robert. We also need to discuss cemeteries."

Dear God, I would have to bury my own children! All of them! Telemarketers occasionally called us trying to sell a cheap cemetery plot, but Melissa and I dismissed those calls and never gave it another thought. Now I had no choice.

He mentioned a cemetery called Glenridge that was out in the country, with gentle hills, trees, and a tranquil lake. This sounded fitting to me. But that was all I could bear to say or discuss at this point. It was excruciating to even think past the autopsies of my children, let alone their funeral and burial at this point.

What about Melissa? I still didn't know where my wife was! Oh, how I missed her and needed her with me.

After Pastor Jerls left, a nurse came to my room with a special surprise—a piano keyboard! I was floored. The staff had learned that I played the piano and knew I was looking for one in the hospital onto which I could pour out my emotions. Since there were none available, this kind woman went home and brought a portable keyboard, stand, and pedal just for me. Having the familiar sight of those keys in front of me felt like someone pouring ointment over my wounds.

The piano had always been a refuge of solitude where I could go to bare my heart. Now I needed to release my emotions in a tangible musical expression. I placed my hands on the keys, as I had done so often over the past 27 years, in no apparent formation—just to see what would come out. Often, my fingers just started dancing on the keys, and a song would soon be born. But not this time.

Nothing.

I couldn't play a thing.

Still, it felt good just to touch the keys. It was a start. At least I was still upright, breathing, and able to press down a few notes. More would have to come later.

I kept thinking of Melissa, worrying about her, hoping I would hear her voice again. But an officer came to my room and said they called off the search for the night and would resume at sunrise the next day. It was getting late, and people were leaving to find hotel rooms for the night. I needed to rest and prepare for the press conference.

Dad and I spoke privately in my room.

"Dad, besides my account of what happened last night, what's your sense of what I should say?"

My father, an extremely wise man, often looked pensively into the distance and drew a deep breath before he would make a statement of conviction. When he did that this time, I knew I should pay close attention to his words.

"Son, this is where the rubber meets the road," he said. "Give it straight. Explain how shattered you are. But don't hesitate to say how you still trust God. This is where we either believe what we say or we don't. Either God is God, or He's not."

He was right, and I knew it.

"Yes. And I want to talk about my family and the wonderful life we lived—the life God blessed us with for so many years."

"Yes, Robert. Talk about them, celebrate them, and urge others to love their families as you have."

My parents were hesitant to leave me at the hospital, but I needed to be alone for awhile—I needed some peace and quiet. I wanted to gather my thoughts and write my statement for the press conference in the morning.

It was nearly 1:00 A.M. when they left. I climbed onto my stiff, sterile hospital bed to formulate words for the press conference. My brother Mark had gone to the store and bought me a small spiral notebook and some notepads to write down all the details, phone numbers, names, and other information from friends and relatives that had started pouring in. Before I began to write, I said a prayer that God would inspire my words and be my Guide. Then I started jotting down whatever words came to my mind.

Finally, after 2:00 A.M., I turned out my light to try to sleep. I drifted off to sleep, utterly exhausted and devastated from what had been—thus far—the worst 24 hours of my life.

7

"God Is My Strength"

I slept a few hours and woke up around 6:00 A.M. on Monday, the first day of September. Surprisingly, I had no nightmares. To me, that was nothing short of God's amazing grace, since there was every reason to have dreadful dreams for the rest of my life.

I stumbled around the room for a bit, staggering as the pain of identifying all four of my children the day before settled in once again. My thoughts went back to Melissa.

As they had the previous day, people started gathering out in the lobby, and the kind hospital staff brought out some breakfast food. I still didn't feel like eating much of anything. Some law-enforcement officers came to my room and gave instructions to me, my parents, Melissa's dad and stepmom, and my pastor on how the press conference was going to flow. The officers were going to escort us to a local hotel in two police cars, usher us to the front of the room, ask me to read my statement at the podium—flanked by my parents and pastor—and then usher us off without allowing questions from the media. The press still didn't know where I was staying, and the police were working hard to keep it that way.

Before we left for the press conference, I excused myself from the

escalating commotion in the lobby so I could pray and add a few
more comments to my notepad.

*Dear God, give me strength, stand with me, give me peace, and help
me say what needs to be said.*

Words to a song that Steven Curtis Chapman wrote after the
terrorist attacks on 9/11 came to my mind: "God is God and I am
not."[1] I felt this would be the most fitting way to open my comments—by establishing our trust in the sovereignty of God, no matter what.

The officers led the six of us down a back hallway in the hospital to their waiting police cars. Within a few minutes, we arrived at
the hotel. The parking lot was littered with news vans and satellite
dishes. Although the sight of so many TV cameras and microphones
would normally have paralyzed me, I was not afraid. I had already
faced my worst fear in the flood and as I had identified my children.

Instead of fear, I felt peace. Instead of anxiety, I felt resolve.
Instead of confusion, I sensed certainty—about my children's reloca-
tion to heaven and about my reunion with them some day. God had
not abandoned me. His promises were still true. I genuinely sensed
His peace and presence about me.

I later realized that this was the moment my new calling in life
began. I was facing and embracing head-on the worst pain of my
life—the worst pain imaginable for a father. While I was undoubt-
edly experiencing post-traumatic stress, I fully realized the magni-
tude of what happened to my family, and I was accepting and dealing
with it. I surrendered my will, and God took over, lifting me to a
level of living I'd never known before.

I allowed Him in. I didn't shut down. I didn't shut God out. It
was purely the miracle of His presence and peace within me. While
I had hoped for a miracle to save my family, and I was still hoping

for a miracle to see Melissa alive, we were all witnessing a living, walking, breathing miracle in the fact that I was even alive and functioning.

I began by thanking the many agencies, volunteers, and medical workers who came together in response to the crisis that claimed my family. And then I came to the core of my message.

"Let me start by saying that 'God is God, and I am not.' The biggest question we have right now is, 'Why?' We don't have an answer, but we have faith and trust in the sovereignty of God.

"I'm only here by the grace of God. I've been told it's a miracle that I'm even alive. God is my strength. God is my refuge, an ever-present help in times of trouble, a shield around about me. God is my glory. He's the lifter of my head.

"I can only do this and get through this through Christ, who gives me strength."

I then recited 2 Corinthians 4:8 (KJV): "We are troubled on every side, yet not distressed; we are perplexed, but not in despair."

I talked about what happened that night—driving through the rushing current, and our final, frantic, fear-filled minutes together. I asked people to pray for Melissa, who was still missing. Then I shifted my focus and cautioned anyone who would listen.

"If there's anything positive that can come from this terrible tragedy, it is to treasure the importance of families . . . to savor every single minute with your spouses and children.

"Hug and kiss them every day—every morning and every evening. Tell them over and over how much you love them. Snuggle with them at bedtime. Place your hand on their heads and bless them every day.

"Nevertheless, 'It is well with my soul.' Even though we're literally walking through the valley of the shadow of death, God's peace that passes all understanding is guarding our hearts and our minds. There is peace in knowing that all four of our children are now with our Lord and Savior, Jesus, in heaven. There is peace in knowing that God is still sovereign and that God is good—all the time. What the devil meant for bad, God will somehow turn into good.

"I feel God reminding me to be still and know that He is good."

I told them about each of my children, and then closed by saying, "We *will* get through this. We *will* rise above this. And by God's grace, *good* will somehow come from this."

As I spoke, I could hear Melissa's dad and his wife sobbing behind me. I could see people weeping in front of me. My voice noticeably broke and quavered several times as I spoke of my children, and of the importance of cherishing and hugging your family every day. All at once, that became my message: to be a beacon of hope for families. I felt like a solitary lighthouse rising above a storm-tossed ocean, beaming with a reminder to cherish your loved ones like you mean it!

I finished my statement and followed the officer out of the hotel. Once outside, my parents, my pastor, and Jere and Judy embraced me. We cried in each other's arms, and they couldn't resist asking questions.

"Robert, that was amazing. How did you do that? Where did you come up with those words?"

The single, simple answer to each one remained the same—God. Beyond the grief of describing the account of the flood in front of national TV cameras, there was this underlying tone of hope and even pride for my children, that their lives were beaming across the national airwaves to reach out and touch millions of viewers and listeners. I sensed a burst of reassurance that it wasn't all in vain.

Another group of individuals came to hug me along the sidewalk next to the police car. I didn't recognize them, but they were Al Larsen's mother and siblings. We shared tears as I learned of their relationship and said, "Al? He was Al? Let me tell you what he did." Up to that point, I didn't even know for certain that Al was missing. I gave them the account of how Al was at Melissa's window trying to figure out a way to help us and ultimately gave his all—the greatest love a person can show a friend, let alone a complete stranger. It was difficult to realize their loss on account of my family, and yet there was comfort and pride in knowing how honorably Al had sacrificed his life for the sake of others.

The police officer gently reminded us that it was time to go. The press could be coming around the corner any moment and might follow us back to the hospital. As the officer let us out of the car in front of the hospital, I shook his hand and embraced him. Then he said something I'll never forget.

"You're an awesome, godly witness," he said, his strong, deep voice cracking.

I was honored to hear such words from a respected officer in uniform. I later learned that as we walked into the hospital lobby, my dad turned around to see the police officer leave. He saw that the officer was saluting us, with tears streaming down his cheeks. Dad knew the significance of this from his days in the army. He stopped and stood facing the officer, and returned his salute. It was a powerful moment of honor and pride in the midst of such horrible grief.

As the day went on, I felt more and more unsettled. Where was Melissa? Was she alive? Was she okay? Why couldn't they find her? I couldn't go anywhere without Melissa. We needed complete closure with all five of my family members before we could do anything else.

My sister Mary and her husband, Jeff, were determined to help. They couldn't just sit around the hospital weeping. They had to do something . . . anything, so they went to the flood site and searched for Melissa on foot.

They walked the full length of the slowly subsiding creek—a full two miles each way—knee-deep in mud, weeds, and sloshing water. They returned hours later with personal belongings they had found inside our van: Zachary's glasses, with the red strap still on them; Melissa's lipstick; Alenah's little doll. The tactile memories these small items evoked seemed to surge into my fingers, through my arms, and down to my toes as my whole body shivered in pain. It was awful, and yet wonderful, to have something of theirs to grasp.

I later learned that my third-oldest brother, George, and his wife and family didn't learn of the flood until Sunday night when they returned from a weekend vacation to their home near Washington, D.C. George immediately flew out Monday morning to our home and met our neighbors Mica and Kerry. They let him into our house, and George shifted into attorney mode and began scouring the house for legal papers, insurance policies, wills, and other papers typically needed when someone dies.

He called State Farm to let them know what had happened. He also tuned one ear to our house phone and the other to his cell phone. The two phones rang incessantly, and he filled an entire notepad with jottings and call logs from national TV networks, grieving friends, neighbors offering to help clean or bring food, relatives needing directions, newspaper reporters, and so on.

One by one that Monday, as the rest of my extended family learned of the news, they reeled in pain and began to compose themselves for the trip to Kansas City. Meanwhile, back in Emporia, the only thing we could do was wait and pray for Melissa. All we could hold on to was hope.

Please, God . . . please . . .

8

"We Found Melissa"

Early Tuesday morning, I heard those footsteps again—the unmistakable sound of leather boots on the hospital hallway floor. Could this be it? Did they finally find my beautiful bride? Could this be the day we would finally be reunited?

Every cell in my body ached to hold Melissa, the love of my life, and just cry with her. I couldn't even imagine what my first words to her would be, or how she would react to the devastating fate of all our children.

The footsteps got louder and closer. They slowed a bit and then turned into my room. I hoped against all hope that it would be good news. I was anxiously anticipating the next words to be uttered, and yet I was dreading them too. I knew another pivotal moment was at hand.

It was the same trooper I had first come to on the highway after emerging from the raging waters, climbing over the barbed wire fence, and struggling up the embankment.

I was already sitting down, so he pulled up a chair and sat close to me. He was holding a navy blue bag. Instantly, I recognized it. It was Melissa's purse! It was caked with dried mud and had a bright orange police identification tag on it.

"Robert, we found Melissa's purse . . ."

I reached out and took it. It felt good just to hold it. When the water had first seeped onto the floorboards on Saturday night, we had stuffed my wallet and other valuables like our handheld GPS into Melissa's purse so we could hang them high on a coat hook in the van to keep them dry. I was so thankful to open my wallet and see all the beautiful pictures of my children. They were still in place behind the transparent plastic picture windows, saturated from muddy river water, but I could make out every face. Now those pictures, which I had shared with business colleagues and customers over the years, were all that remained of my children.

There were also some water-stained dollar bills in my wallet, plus a stained note from Makenah—tucked behind my vehicle insurance card—that read: "I Love yow Dadey. Yow R the grat Dadey. Love Makenah."

Oh, how that note pierced my heart. In the midst of another powerful gush of grief, I struggled to focus my attention on something inanimate that I could remain in control of. I pulled the GPS out of Melissa's purse and held it in my hands. I fumbled with it and ran my fingers over the buttons and display. It appeared to be in good mechanical shape. I pressed the On button out of utter futility. Of course, nothing happened.

I said something completely inappropriate and unrelated to this moment of grief, but it was something tangible that the logical engineering side of my brain could latch on to. It was as if my mind needed something—anything—to digest and comprehend. Everything over the past three days had been inconceivable and incomprehensible. I

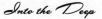

needed something I could control, since the rest of my world had fallen apart.

"I was wondering if there was any chance that this GPS even survived. It's supposed to be water-resistant up to three feet. Maybe before it stopped working, it tracked and recorded the path of our van in the flood. Maybe that could help us find out . . ."

I'm sure it sounded strange to him. I was struggling to divert my attention to something technical and tangible to avoid what I suspected he was going to say next. He was trying to be as gentle and compassionate as he could, but there was no way to escape the real reason for his visit:

". . . and we found Melissa."

I instantly knew by the tone of his voice and the look in his eyes that Melissa had not survived. I heard him, but I didn't want to listen to those words. More than anything, I wanted to clamp his mouth shut and keep those words from coming out. All I managed to do was fiddle with that broken GPS in my hands and utter some ridiculous comment about it, as if I didn't even hear him.

But I couldn't avoid the inevitable, and it slowly, painfully hit me: Melissa, my bride, was gone. They were gone—my children, my wife . . . my family.

It was all over. Melissa, the love of my life, was truly gone for good. *Oh, God, help me! What do I do? How can I possibly go on? They took everything except for a tiny fragment of my heart with them to heaven.*

And yet, even then, there was comfort in knowing that my heart and my family were all safely protected in heaven. After three days of wondering, waiting, and searching, I was relieved to know where Melissa was and what had ultimately happened to her.

I can do this, I thought. *With God's strength and grace, I can bear this. I'm thankful that neither Melissa nor our children need to bear this cross. I'm thankful I don't need to explain it to any of them. I don't need to be strong for them. All I need to do now is just stay alive and upright and functioning.*

The trooper spoke again, returning my attention to the moment at hand.

"We'll have her body here in a few hours for you to identify," he said.

"Okay," was all I could manage in reply. "Thanks, Officer."

I hugged him out of gratitude for all he had done, out of relief, and now out of the overwhelming sense of closure I felt after all that had transpired since I had first come to him after emerging from the floodwaters.

As he was leaving, I asked him if I could visit the flood site before I left for home. I believed that I needed to come to grips, face-to-face, with the place where my family had died. I had to face the fear. I had to see for myself where and how all this had happened. It had been so dark, so noisy, so difficult to believe as it unfolded. I knew there would still be media in the area, plus emergency vehicles and even road repair vehicles. I wanted a police escort for protection. He agreed to look into it.

I followed him out and made my way to the lobby where everyone was anxiously waiting for news of Melissa. They, like me, had been unsure what to do until we learned of her fate. Now I needed to let everyone know.

I approached my parents in the hallway and motioned for them to follow me. Just by the look in my eyes, they understood. They knew what the trooper had just told me. We headed toward Jere in the lobby. Judy was by his side. With the five of us in a small circle, I took a deep breath and opened my mouth.

"They found Melissa."

I took another deep breath and struggled with how to finish these words, with what to say.

"She's in heaven with our children."

I could see the hope dissipate from Jere's face and devastation replace it.

"Jere, I'm sorry. She didn't make it." My voice gave way and tears gushed again. "I'm so sorry."

Everyone else began sobbing too. Mom and Dad were visibly crushed. Ever since the day more than 13 years earlier when I had first introduced Melissa to Mom and Dad during Easter of 1990, they had had an instant natural bond, almost as if she were already a member of the family.

Jere took the news particularly hard since Melissa was his only daughter. They had endured many tough times in their lives— working relentlessly on the family farm during Melissa's childhood, then enduring the stress and hardship of bankruptcy on account of the farm, followed soon after by her parents' divorce when she was in high school. After the divorce, Melissa had continued living with her mother until she graduated from high school. And soon after graduating, Melissa had moved out on her own to Boston.

But over the past six years, since we had moved to Kansas City, Melissa and her father had reconnected and strengthened their relationship. She cherished his approval and wanted to please him.

Jere had hoped for three agonizing days that his daughter would come bouncing through those elevator doors and into our arms on the third floor of the hospital. Three days earlier, despite the grim events and bleak outlook, his eyes were full of hope and intently locked on the elevator doors like a hawk. Now it would never happen. Jere wept hard.

The five of us hugged each other through our tears. Eventually, I made my way back to my room alone. It was time to finally leave this hospital. Three days had come and gone, and I still hadn't shaved or showered. I went to the bathroom and splashed water on my face. I started gathering my belongings, since we would be heading home soon.

I took a deep breath, knowing that much still remained ahead of me: identifying Melissa, going to the flood site, driving two hours home, and setting foot into my home for the first time—alone. My new life and my new identity had already begun.

I needed something into which I could pour my welling emotions. Drawn to the familiar comfort of the keyboard, I placed my hands on it to see what would come. I played an A-flat minor chord up in a high register—like a sad funeral bell that had just rung. I played it again, as if it was tolling to mourn their deaths. Over and over I played it. It was the genesis of an instrumental composition I eventually titled "Behold, My Family" to try to capture the overwhelming emotion of identifying their bodies.

Other than tears, it was the first outward expression of grief that I was able to formulate. I couldn't write down any words yet. Only music could come close to capturing my emotions.

Malcolm had found and given to me a copy of the hymn I asked him for: "It Is Well with My Soul," written by Horatio Spafford after his four children drowned in the Atlantic Ocean in 1873. I now placed the copy in front of me on the keyboard stand. I stared at the words for awhile and digested their ironic similarity to my own life.

When sorrows like sea billows roll—
Whatever my lot, Thou hast taught me to say,
It is well, it is well with my soul.[1]

I played and gently sang the song to myself, grief infusing every syllable, every phrase, every note. Perhaps the most consoling portion of the song was the last verse, which begins, "And, Lord, haste the day when my faith shall be sight, the clouds be rolled back as a scroll . . ." That gave me hope. My entire body strained for that glorious day when I'd be reunited with my family.

I wanted it to be here *now*. I wanted to be in heaven *now*. I wished I were with my family. But even though I no longer wanted to be on this earth, I never considered taking my own life. I just longed to be joined to my family.

Yet I could sense that God had a profound purpose for my life. Already I could see that people's lives were being touched in a positive way. I felt that God had kept me alive for a reason.

A few hours passed, and then someone came to me and said, "It's time, Mr. Rogers." Our parents, my pastor, and a couple of my siblings came with me. We were led slowly down that same long hallway to the emergency room area. We walked in tandem, arms locked. This was the third time I had made the trip down this hallway to identify the body of someone I loved. It was the first time for most of the others who were with me. We entered the same small examination room where I had identified Makenah two days earlier.

Before coming downstairs, we had learned that Melissa had been found two miles from the highway in a retention pond that had tripled in size to nearly 100 acres of water. It took three days for the water to recede enough for her body to be found. One of the search dogs had picked up her scent and led the rescue workers in a boat to where she was. I learned later that they had found the body of Al Larsen, the man who had tried to save us, not far from Melissa. The force of the current evidently carried their bodies to the same general area in the retention pond. They found Melissa around 7:00 A.M.

The smell of the muddy river water, coupled with the unmistakable odor of death, was almost too much for us to bear as we crammed into the tiny examination room. But worst of all was the heartrending sight of the first girl I truly fell in love with and faithfully pledged myself to on New Year's Eve nearly 12 years earlier. There she was, on the table in front of me: lifeless, still, completely silent. The contagious bounce in her step and radiance of her face that illuminated her world were gone.

Yet there was a real peace about her. Perhaps that peace was there because she was with all of our children in heaven. Maybe it was there because God had honored her wish to never leave them again. I collapsed over her body and groaned. I felt as though I was about to vomit.

My mind whirled dizzily with unspoken words for my wife.

Melissa. Melissa. Melissa. My love. My life. My friend. How could you be gone too? How, so soon? Why? We never even got to say goodbye . . . no last kiss . . . no last hug . . . no last "I love you" or "I'll see you." It seems like just yesterday that you first flashed your beautiful smile my way. I loved you more than I ever imagined I could possibly love someone.

We were supposed to grow old together. It's not supposed to end like this. Not now. We overcame so many trials to get this far and raise four beautiful children.

We wanted to spend the rest of our lives making memories together. Melissa. Please don't leave me, my love. I'm completely alone now. It's just me. What am I supposed to do without you? I need you here, by my side . . .

I mentally pleaded with God to somehow change what had happened.

Please, God, don't let it be so. Please, please, please, God. My bride—the gorgeous girl You gave me—handpicked by You—divinely placed in my life. All of our children, too. Why? Why, God? Why? We trusted You! We trusted You to protect us! Father, God, why? Why?

The more I pleaded with God as I held Melissa, the more I sounded like a wounded child.

It hurts so badly. Please, please help me. I can't do this, Father. I can't. God, it hurts. It's all too much.

God, I need You as I've never needed You before. But, Lord, I feel betrayed—as if You built us up only to tear us down. I'm so disappointed. I'm so let down. I don't feel as though I can trust You anymore. Everything You've given me, You've taken away. Why? For no reason You turned my world upside down.

You were the One who formed our beautiful family into who we were. You were faithful to us through childbirths, miscarriages, disabilities, and adoption. And through it all, we chose to remain faithful to You.

But now it was all gone, and I didn't understand.

What have I done so wrong that You should be so cruel to me? I asked God. *Why did You leave me behind on this earth to bear this horror alone? Why have You crushed everything that was right in my life with such an unexplainable wrong? I don't know if I can trust You now, Lord. I really don't know. I really don't want to. I really don't feel like trusting You anymore.*

But even as those thoughts were racing through my mind, I knew I would have to trust God, if for no other reason than because past experience and simple obedience told me to. The only other real choice I had was to turn and run away. People would understand after what I'd just been through. But what good could come from that?

I told God that I would trust Him for the next 60 seconds. And that if I could make it through all 60 of them, I would trust Him for another 60 seconds. And another. The minutes would eventually become hours, and the hours would turn into days. As painful as it was, I knew I would have to choose once again to remain faithful to Him and put my trust in Him alone. I knew there was nowhere else I could really turn for true comfort.

I don't know how long I wept or how long my protestations to God lasted, but eventually I lifted my head and gently brought my lips up to Melissa's face to kiss her one last time. I placed my left hand on her head and my right hand over hers, and I surrendered Melissa to heaven as I had my children.

That moment marked the beginning of having to let go of my entire family. Everyone else drifted aimlessly into the hallway in shock. I hovered over Melissa and said, "Bubby, thanks for all the memories. Thanks for all the ice cream. I love you, Melissa."

2

Return to Jacob Creek

I t felt strange to be traveling on the highway again without Melissa or any of our children with me. Within a few minutes, our procession of vehicles approached milepost 116 on the turnpike. We descended into the valley of the shadow of death—into the place where all the rain had collected just three nights earlier. It simply didn't look possible that so much water could have collected in such a tranquil and verdant place as these gently rolling hills.

The sun was shining brightly, such a contrast to the last time I had been on this highway. Yet scars from that dark Saturday night remained. The highway was littered with construction equipment repaving the portion of the road that had been washed away and replacing the 11 concrete medians swept from the highway. The traffic was limited to one lane in each direction. The head police car led us past the dip where our van had stalled, past the construction equipment, and over to the right shoulder. My sister Anne's pickup truck followed slowly behind us.

After the caravan parked, we rushed toward each other and embraced.

"Robert," she said, struggling to get the words out, "your family made everything they did . . . sacred."

She fell to her knees on the embankment. The tall grass was noticeably flattened in one direction. I moved down the muddy, grassy embankment, closer to the culvert opening near the pool of water that was now peacefully still. I fell facedown on the ground and wept over the spot where my family had died. As I held on to the grass, I thought of Saturday night and how I had longed to hold on to each of my family members and keep them from drowning— but couldn't.

I felt that I needed to touch the water. It had been so menacing, so deadly . . . and now it was so still. I couldn't let it control me. I got up from the ground and inched toward the water's edge. I knelt on one knee and saw my reflection. I slowly slipped my fingertips into the water until my hands were submerged. I felt tingles permeate my body through my fingers, up my arms, and down to my toes—as if my family were reaching out and imparting one last breath of their life and strength through me. I didn't want the feeling to end, but as quickly as it entered me, I felt it slip away—back into the water.

That was it. They were gone.

Others were having their own private moments, coming to grips with what happened on that spot. Anne was singing some of the songs I had written for my children over the years.

The rest of us joined her in singing a lullaby I had written that all my siblings had learned through my children. In the midst of such utter devastation, it seemed strange to sing words about God's plans for our children's lives being so great. For years we had firmly believed that we were instilling God's Word into our children to guide them

in His ways through their lifetimes. Now those years suddenly felt
fruitless and senseless. As if they had all been for nothing.

How could this possibly be God's plan? How could this ever be
construed as His perfect will? What went wrong? Why?

So many questions lingered. No answers came. Yet the music of
my family's childhood memories still brought solace and comfort.

Again, I had to release and surrender my family, despite the hurt
and the unanswered questions. I willingly pursued the pain in that
water and dove even further into the darkness. As I did, I discovered
an even deeper peace and grace of God. By facing that harsh and
painful reality, I found that it couldn't control me and didn't have a
hold on me. I was still breathing. I was still moving. My heart was
still beating.

As I released my family to God, I surrendered myself into His
grip. There in the darkness—in the security of God's palm—was
where I found the strength and refuge of His abiding peace. I stood
up and took a deep breath.

We solemnly made our way back to the cars. The police escorted
us southbound to a normally restricted overpass so that we could
turn around and head north back to Emporia.

We met at the Golden Corral and ate, paying for it with money
donated by employees of the hotel where my family had stayed. It
felt good to be among family and even hear a few laughs. We needed
that. We needed to breathe, eat, and know that we could still laugh
again. We formulated our plans for the two-hour ride to our home
in Liberty. But first, I had to stop at the Kansas Turnpike Authority
station near the Emporia tollbooth to recover items retrieved by
rescue personnel during their careful search of the flood area. The
authorities had also requested a copy of my press conference notes—
for a written statement.

The trooper I had seen on the turnpike the night of the flood was there and was once again very gentle and kind with us. He showed us the accumulated belongings from the flood wreckage. I immediately spotted my children's red Radio Flyer All-Terrain Wagon. We always kept it in the back of the van, ready to use at any time. The wheels were now caked with mud. It felt good to see it and touch it again. It represented a wealth of memories with my family.

I needed a half-hour to transcribe by hand all the jumbled notes from my press conference onto the police report ledger. It was quiet in the turnpike station as my pen scratched across the paper. The only sound I heard was the occasional interruption of the scanner radio. After finishing my report and handing it to the trooper, I hugged him one last time.

I went outside to meet my family—all waiting patiently by their cars for me. We loaded up and finally left Emporia. It was early evening by now, and it would be dark by the time we got home.

Home . . .

Where was home now? What was home now? What awaited me? Did I really have a home? Could it really be my home without Melissa, Makenah, Zachary, Nicholas, and Alenah? I knew that after I arrived, I would have to enter into the deep darkness once again.

The two-hour ride home along I-35 was mostly a blur. My mind and body were utterly exhausted from the nonstop emotions and personal demands of the past three days. But as we traveled through downtown Kansas City and approached our suburb, I thought of all the times over the past three years that I had raced home from Wichita or Independence, Kansas, eager to see my family and meet them at the door.

Tonight, after the worst three days of my life, I was again coming home from Wichita—but this time to an empty house. I had no idea what awaited me. I only knew that none of my family was waiting there for me.

Nothing could prepare me for this moment. In the glow of the streetlights, I could see the long line of forsythia bushes that Melissa and I had planted along the retaining wall of our property. They nicely barricaded our home with a layer of privacy from all the street traffic. At the end of the retaining wall, we turned right onto the side street to enter our driveway. I could see several police cars at the northeast and southeast corners of our property. I assumed they were there to keep the press and other onlookers away.

Then I saw it: The grassy island inside our half-circle driveway had been transformed into a glistening, glimmering memorial to my family. Candles, balloons, flowers, bears, stuffed animals, cards, angels, figurines, soccer balls, dance shoes, and all sorts of memorabilia. In the darkness, the island was aglow with warm flickering lights. It was remarkable.

There were so many cars in our procession that some had to pull onto the grass to keep the driveway clear. We parked in the driveway where family, friends, and neighbors had gathered in the darkness. As I emerged from the car, they immediately moved toward us all. I embraced my brother George who had arrived the day before. We squeezed each other tighter than ever before and said, simply, "I love you, bro."

In between hugs with other relatives, I was trying to locate my best friends, Janet and Kirk. Finally, we spotted one another and met in a tearful embrace.

I made my way over to the huge memorial and was awed by the outpouring of love and compassion for my family. There were so many notes and cards.

I needed to step inside our home. I dreaded the moment, but I knew I had to do it. We were facing the garage door, which was open. There was a noticeable gap where our van belonged. For a moment, I wished Melissa was just at the store with the kids and would return at any moment and pull into her usual spot. Oh, how I wanted that to be so.

I slowly walked up the front walkway past the flower garden and trellis that Melissa had so meticulously designed and finished that summer. I approached the front porch, noticing the huge white railing with more than 100 spindles I had built around the perimeter, closely spaced at Melissa's request to keep our children safe. I also noticed the white swing Melissa had painted, where we spent many summer nights rocking gently. We loved that porch. It was about six feet wide and forty feet long. Normally, it was very homey and welcoming. Now, however, it only reinforced the absence of the rest of my family.

I ascended the single step to the porch. The screen door creaked when I opened it with my left hand. As I grabbed the front doorknob with my right hand, it felt like a surge of electricity was running through my body. I turned the knob, leaned into the heavy door to force it open, and stepped across the threshold.

All at once it hit me like a wave across my face.

I could smell them.

I could smell my family.

10

Back Home

E very home and every family have a distinct "scent." Ours was a sweet aroma to me—one that screamed of happiness, kids, and family. It was a mixture of pizza, ice cream, popcorn, baby powder, chocolate-chip cookies, semisweet delights, and true love.

Others commented on the warmth and joy they felt when they entered our home. On the day Melissa and I had moved in, back in April 1997, we had formed a circle with her family in the front entryway and dedicated our home to God, praying that His anointing would touch every person who entered. God honored that prayer. My friend Janet once remarked that being in our home was like being "in the lap of God."

As I stood in my home for the first time since the flood, the essence of my family engulfed me. Reminders of them surrounded me. But there was something else to remind me that they were gone: silence. There were no cheers as I came through the door, no cries in the other room, no whining over who pinched whom, no "I love yous," and no music.

The absence of noise was like a slap in the face.

My gut tightened with a sickening feeling that had become all too familiar by now—as though I needed to purge from my body all the emotion that was welling up within me. I closed my eyes and slowly took a deep breath.

I could sense my family's presence all around. They seemed so close, yet utterly out of reach. Without the grace of God, it would have been unbearable. Everyone around me seemed frozen in place . . . watching me . . . wondering if I was going to collapse from the enormity of the moment.

In front of me, I saw the steps ascending to the second floor— lined with all four of our children's earliest baby pictures—steps that our kids would have been gleefully spilling down by now just to greet me. To the left, I saw the dining room where we shared so many meals, memories, and holidays with relatives on the elegant Queen Anne table with the faded and noticeably worn seat cushions. To the right, I saw the living room with the grand piano. That was the most difficult room to see.

That was where our children merrily played and sang nearly every night before bedtime. My grandmother in Cincinnati, who played the piano her entire life and devoted her final years to music therapy at veteran's hospitals until she died in 1995, had lovingly bequeathed her gorgeous 1900 Steinway grand piano to us. Melissa and I had carefully saved up the money to have it refurbished.

The piano had always been a focal point in our home. My children would sing and dance, sometimes colliding with each other, as I would play. At times, it seemed the room would burst at the seams with joy.

I just couldn't believe that all those moments were over. I wanted to keep making memories for years to come, and even experience our grandkids doing the same things our kids did. Melissa and I wanted to live in this home the rest of our lives. That's why we bought it—for a lifetime of family memories.

Our bed was temporarily in the living room since we had been remodeling our upstairs bedroom over the summer months. I was drawn to it first, and I slowly inched toward Melissa's side. Next to the bed was a book on homeschooling that she had just started reading since we had set up a classroom in the basement so she could begin teaching Makenah and Nicholas. I sat on her side of the bed, picked up the book, and buried my face in it. That's when I broke down.

"Melissa! Melissa!" was all I could cry out, over and over.

I just couldn't believe she was gone. I collapsed into her pillow and could smell her fragrance. Lying on her side of the bed, the realization hit me vividly: I would never have the chance to cuddle next to Melissa, kiss her cheek, gently touch her arm, be intimate with her, or fall asleep by her side.

Never again.

I slowly proceeded through the entire house and mourned each of my children all over again—every room, every aroma, every bed, every pillow—the smell of baby wipes and baby powder that still lingered from Alenah's crib; the ballet posters and slippers in Makenah's room; the Superman capes near Zachary's bed; the monogrammed Winnie the Pooh blanket on Nicholas's bed; the fresh bath towels hanging on the wall pegs; the tubby toys in the bucket next to the bathtub; dishes in the sink and artwork on the kitchen cabinets.

The videos we had watched on Friday night were near the TV in the family room. There, just beyond the step from the kitchen into the family room, was the small blue backpack we had overlooked on our way out the door Saturday morning—the one with our boys' socks and spare clothes that Melissa was frantically searching for in the van just before the wedding. That fleeting moment seemed like a lifetime ago now, even though it had been less than four days.

Tears spilled down my face again.

Could I still dare to hope through all of this? It felt as though God had given me gallons of sorrows to drink, and I was gulping it all at once. I was exhausted and weary. My abdomen ached from all the crying. A pain in the pit of my stomach never seemed to go away.

I couldn't sleep in our bed. I just wasn't ready for that. What could I handle? Probably not in the boys' room—not just yet. I needed a small, private space to be alone.

Makenah's room. Yes, that felt right. Her room was small, but cozy and comforting. I went upstairs to her room and closed the door behind me. I noticed the butterflies suspended from her ceiling that Melissa had made out of tissue and construction paper for one of Makenah's school parties.

I melted at the sight of a paper where she had drawn a great big smiley face of herself along with the words "God loves me!" I was so thankful she knew that God indeed loved her. Evidently, Melissa and I had succeeded in conveying that to her through our words and actions.

Well done, Melissa.

I finally managed to turn off the light and curl up under the pink sheets—covered with clouds, rainbows, and the words "Sweet Dreams"—we had just given Makenah three weeks before for her birthday. I stared at the ceiling where, out of the darkness, I could see the glow-in-the-dark stars we had stuck up there years before. I thought of all the times I lay next to her, reading to her, reciting Scripture, and just talking about the day. It hurt like a knife jammed into my heart, yet I was grateful for all those memories.

I cried myself to sleep.

Sweet dreams, Makenah. Sweet dreams.

I was able to sleep deeply and soundly for a few hours and woke up around 3:00 A.M. Completely disoriented, I looked around to get a handle on where I was. It took me awhile to realize that I was back at home, in Makenah's room, in her bed—and that my family was gone.

I cried into her pillow and prayed for God's hands to wrap around me again and sustain me with His strength. I clung to and repeatedly prayed the verses we had leaned on throughout our marriage and our challenges with Zachary's Down syndrome: "I can do all things through Christ who strengthens me" (Philippians 4:13, NKJV), and "My grace is sufficient for you, for my power is made perfect in weakness" (2 Corinthians 12:9).

I needed God's grace and strength now more than ever. I was physically and emotionally empty. Yet the week ahead of me would be formidable.

"Please, God, give me *Your* strength. Give me *Your* peace. I need You, Lord." I prayed and opened my Bible to the Book of Psalms. I flipped through a few pages and came to Psalm 18.

> I love you, O LORD, my strength. The LORD is my rock, my fortress and my deliverer; my God is my rock, in whom I take refuge. He is my shield and the horn of my salvation, my stronghold. I call to the LORD, who is worthy of praise, and I am saved. . . . The cords of death entangled me; the torrents of destruction overwhelmed me. The cords of the grave coiled around me; the snares of death confronted me. In my distress I called to the LORD; I cried to my God for help. From his temple he heard my

voice; my cry came before him, into his ears. The earth
trembled and quaked. . . . He parted the heavens and
came down; dark clouds were under his feet. . . . He made
darkness his covering, his canopy around him—the dark
rain clouds of the sky. . . . He reached down from on high
and took hold of me; he drew me out of deep waters. . . .
He brought me out into a spacious place; he rescued me
because he delighted in me. . . . You, O LORD, keep my
lamp burning; my God turns my darkness into light.
(selected verses)

I found my laptop and opened the lid. I needed to prepare my
comments for a local press conference that our mayor and my family had arranged for later that day at our church. I wanted to thank
all the Kansas rescue workers and share how they found Melissa. I
typed for about 45 minutes, telling the story of how Melissa and I
met in Boston and what a wonderful wife and mother she was.
When I was finished, I closed the computer, lay back in Makenah's
bed against her pillow, and just stared at the ceiling.

I thought back over my life—growing up in Cincinnati,
meeting Melissa in Boston, the births of our children. I let myself
remember . . .

11

Looking Back

We never had a big house or lots of toys as I was growing up, and we rarely went out to eat—not even to McDonald's. As the youngest of eight children, I wore the hand-me-downs that had survived my older brothers. A hot shower was a luxury, simply because the older siblings had used up all the hot water by the time it was my turn. I didn't complain—that's just the way it is in large families.

Mom stayed home with us until we were all in school. Then she went to college and earned her bachelor's and master's degrees in education. She even took me to her classes at the University of Cincinnati when I was little.

Dad worked hard in broadcasting at the ABC and PBS affiliates in Cincinnati, and later in sales. After a full day of work, he taught at Xavier University and the University of Cincinnati. He took courses at night and on weekends and earned his bachelor's and master's degrees. He showed us what persistence was: It took him 12 years just to get his bachelor's degree!

With such a large family, my parents had to be creative to make ends meet. Mom would buy dented canned goods for a dollar a box at the grocery store. We'd then have fun guessing what was for dinner by shaking the cans that had no labels on the outside. My dad would buy 100 loaves of bread for $10 at a time. It was only 10 cents a loaf! We'd form an assembly line at the kitchen table to make sandwiches for school lunches.

My parents made sure we had a camping vacation every year and that everyone got *something* for Christmas, even if it was little more than socks and underwear. Because we grew up with very few luxuries, my siblings and I had a deep sense of gratitude for simple things in life.

We all attended parochial school, and Mass was a cornerstone of our daily lives—even on Saturdays. If we misbehaved at church, and every one of us did at one point or another, we were pulled from the pews and taken to the back for a good scolding. We learned to listen and surrender our will to loving authority figures: our parents. We learned at an early age that "It's not about me."

My parents' emphasis on obedience and discipline, balanced with love and grace, made an impression on me to be a good student in school, even during my earliest years. Good grades didn't come naturally, but I worked hard for them because I wanted to please my teachers and my parents.

Music lifted me too. It had always been a big part of our family. All of my siblings played some musical instrument, and Mom would often sing refrains around the house. We had an old, monstrous upright piano in our family room that my older siblings took lessons and practiced on. Then Grandma Rogers found us a baby grand that we put in the living room. I was seven when I watched Dad teach some of the others a song on that piano. I was enamored with the jazzy beat of "In the Mood" and the way Dad's fingers danced across the keys. Eventually, I mustered up the courage to tap his arm and say, "Can I try?"

"Well, sure, my son."

Following his lead, I spread my small hands across the enormous keys, and almost immediately, I picked up both patterns in each hand. My fingers had found a home with the piano. It was as if it became an extension of me.

My parents soon recognized that I had a special talent, so they signed me up for piano lessons at age 10 at the University of Cincinnati's College-Conservatory of Music. I was a painfully shy boy, and playing the piano in front of others was difficult for me—whether it was at a nursing home or at large family gatherings. But I had to overcome my shyness so that I could play. Looking back, I could see how that time was "breaking" me of me—forcing me to let go of my ego—so that my gifts could be shared for the benefit of many.

I was never part of the "in" crowd in school. In fact, from the third grade on I was teased and called names for no apparent reason—except, perhaps, that I got good grades and played the piano. Being a sensitive kid, I took the rejection and verbal abuse that much harder. When we picked teams during gym or for dodgeball on the playground, I was usually one of the last ones chosen. I was never invited to the weekend parties. I was crushed and hurt by such rejection from my peers, and I responded by pouring myself into my schoolwork, service activities, and music.

A turning point for me came in the seventh grade when I was asked to play a piano solo in the annual glee-club concert. It would be a medley of three songs I had memorized. But in a gymnasium packed with hundreds of parents and relatives, I was so nervous I blanked out on which notes to play. My fingers kept moving in the correct relative rhythm, but their position on the keyboard had shifted, and something utterly horrendous emerged—like a tinny honky-tonk sound from an untuned barroom piano.

My father had always taught us to finish what we started, so I kept playing and eventually found my way back to the right keys. Gradually, I started to relax. When I hit the finale, I felt as though I was in my element. To my amazement, the entire room erupted into applause while I was still playing. When I finished, the room once again burst into applause. As I stood up and took a bow, my heart felt as though it were ready to burst through my chest. I had found my calling in life: I wanted to be a musician.

I began playing for weddings, including those of all my siblings. I played for special songs at church, for school musicals, recitals, auditions, and Broadway shows for community theater. I also worked as a musical director for a group called the Mini-Mummers.

I started dating in high school but was terribly uncomfortable being myself around girls. I eventually began dating a girl named Trish, whom I met in a community theater production of *Pippin* in Newport, Kentucky. She played the female lead. Our common love of music and the arts put me at ease around her. Like most high-school students, I had become uncomfortable around my parents. They were adjusting to major changes in their lives, going from eight children at home down to just two, and finally only one by my junior year.

I wasn't the stereotypical rebellious child during my high-school years. I wasn't promiscuous with girls, I never did any drugs, I never smoked, and I didn't drink. I knew those vices were wrong, and it seemed pointless to even consider trying them.

My parents had laid a solid moral foundation through their admonitions, their example, and our upbringing in the Catholic faith. Ironically, my only "rebellion" had to do with my faith. Many of my siblings were caught up in the Jesus movement on their college campuses in the 1970s. They read and studied the Bible. My sister Ellen gave me a Bible, and for the first time in my life, I started reading it on my own.

I began to question and test the tenets of my Catholic faith; I felt there had to be more beyond all the traditions and rituals. I was hungry for something deeper with God. I desired more than just the rote daily Catholic Mass. I felt as if I was reciting my faith rather than living it. I had always loved God and loved being at church, but I still felt emptiness within me.

It was a time that forged and defined my faith. The end of high school was in sight, and the separation from my parents was imminent. I wanted to find out what I was made of. I ached to be defined by more than just being a good musician and a good student.

Trish's mom, Angela, attended a small interdenominational church in Newport, Kentucky, named Christian Tabernacle. Trish and I started attending there together every Sunday. I felt very comfortable and was challenged by the teaching of the pastor, Reverend Jack Bishop. One Sunday, when I was 16, he talked about having a "personal" relationship with Jesus Christ.

I had prayed and talked to Jesus many times during my childhood. I had been through baptism, first communion, and confirmation in my Catholic upbringing. But when Reverend Bishop asked, "If today were your last day on earth, would you go to heaven?" I couldn't answer yes. I really wasn't sure. He explained from Scripture that "it is by grace you have been saved, through faith—and this not from yourselves, it is the gift of God—not by works, so that no one can boast" (Ephesians 2:8–9).

I had always believed that if I did enough good deeds and

attended church, I would slide into heaven. But now I wasn't so sure. And I had just heard Reverend Bishop read, "If you confess with your mouth, 'Jesus is Lord,' and believe in your heart that God raised him from the dead, you will be saved" (Romans 10:9).

As part of my Catholic faith, I already believed these things. But I felt I had never personally confessed them outwardly, nor intentionally committed my life to Christ in front of others. Sure, I had recited the Apostles' Creed during Mass hundreds and hundreds of times by then. It fully articulated our belief in Christ's death and resurrection. But I had been reciting something all my life out of obligation.

When Reverend Bishop invited us forward to commit our lives to Christ, I took a step of faith out into the aisle and walked up to the front of the small church with fewer than 20 pews and 75 people. The pastor led me in a personal prayer, and I repeated the words aloud. His daughter, Nicki, was softly playing the organ in the background. When I was done, the pastor turned me around to face the congregation.

Many people were wiping tears from their eyes. I wasn't tearful or shaking or even tingling. I didn't feel any different physically. But I was smiling broadly. It all felt very natural to me and merely affirmed what I already knew to be true about Jesus Christ.

Yet it proved to be a pivotal moment in my life as I figuratively drove a stake into the ground in front of God and others and declared, "I believe in Jesus, I receive His gift of salvation, and I want to live the rest of my life for Him."

Trish and I continued dating many years, and we felt compelled to try to stay together into college. We were both accepted at Anderson College in Anderson, Indiana. It appealed to me because I wanted to major in music, and Anderson had a strong music program with a Christian emphasis.

I now felt it was time to be further committed to Trish. I proposed to her the summer before our sophomore year, and she accepted. I was glad to be more committed to her, but strangely, I wasn't ecstatic. My heart wasn't jumping for joy. It was as though something just wasn't right. Still, we had dated so long that it just seemed like the next natural progression for us. I quickly discovered that I wasn't the only one who wasn't ecstatic. My parents and close friends weren't either. I could sense that they felt we weren't right for each other. I wanted their heartfelt approval but had to settle for reluctant, lukewarm acceptance, and it hurt.

In 1986, after two years of intense musical and computer science study, I made the decision to drop out of music at Anderson and transfer to electrical engineering at the University of Cincinnati. For months I had been pondering over the fact that I wasn't feeling challenged enough in math and science at Anderson and that I was starting to get fed up with practicing the piano for three to six hours every day, cooped up in a small practice room.

I wanted to have a big family someday, and as best I could tell, a career as a music teacher was not going to make a very stable living for a large family. I knew I could still take lessons and play piano around town. I didn't need a degree or a piece of paper to say I could do that.

At first my parents were stunned. From their point of view, it meant that I wasn't going to finish what I had started at Anderson. Dad was always an advocate of finishing what you start. My decision was a huge departure from what he preached to us. Furthermore, it would take five more years to complete an engineering degree because it included 18 months of a co-op internship in the curriculum. Including the two years I'd already spent at Anderson, it would take me a full seven years to earn my bachelor's degree.

But the benefits of my transferring to the University of Cincinnati, such as lower state tuition and being much closer to home, softened their reaction. It was a bold move on my part. It took a great deal of courage to change majors and essentially start over. But looking back, it was clear that the Holy Spirit was gently directing me by prompting my heart. I had an uneasy feeling at Anderson, as if I just didn't have any peace there. I had to go where the peace was.

From then on, that concept became a tenet of my life: Go where the peace is.

12

The Beauty from Kansas

The electrical engineering curriculum at the University of Cincinnati was tremendously demanding. People told me that if you could finish a degree in electrical engineering, you could go on to do anything. After a couple of years of grueling basic courses, it was time to interview for co-op jobs. I accepted a position with Digital Equipment Corporation near Boston. I was drawn to the charm and romance of a big city on the East Coast, full of adventure.

I was still engaged to Trish, but our relationship had grown stagnant. She had transferred from Anderson to Northern Kentucky University when I transferred to the University of Cincinnati. We had no firm plans to marry, and I didn't see her much because of my intense studies.

In March of 1988, I left Cincinnati and headed east for six months of co-op. I had made arrangements to share an apartment with three other guys in Marlborough, Massachusetts, a suburb about an hour west of Boston.

There I was, designing submicron semiconductors for a liquid-nitrogen-cooled, high-speed advanced microprocessor during the day and cooped up at night with three beer-guzzling, couch-potato engineers in a small apartment.

Some adventure.

It became very boring, very fast. I didn't drink beer, and I couldn't stand just sitting around watching movies every night. The biggest adventure we had taken so far was to drive up to New Hampshire, where there was no sales tax, to buy a new TV for the apartment. Yawn. One weekend I said, "Guys, come on. Let's go *do* something. Let's go into the city."

In downtown Boston, we spotted a sidewalk café where a gentleman was playing tunes on a baby grand piano. I stood there for a while and was enamored with the fun he was having, playing songs as the crowd sang along.

When he took a break to grab a soda from the bar, I took a chance.

"Hi, I'm Robert. I play the piano and was wondering if you ever need people to substitute or fill in here from time to time."

"Sure," he replied in a cool music tone—a vernacular I was not fluent speaking. "Why don't you go over and play something for me?"

Suddenly, this was my audition. As I walked to the piano, my mind scrambled to think of the right tune to play off the top of my head. I didn't want to blow it. The festive atmosphere inspired me to play a fast ragtime piece. I followed it with a slower love song. To my amazement, people applauded after I finished playing! I walked back over to the piano player, whose name was Brian, and he said, "Cool. Give me your number, and I'll give you a call."

Thus began a new season of adventures in my life. From then on, Brian called me again and again to play piano at Lily's Sidewalk

Café in Quincy Market. I played piano for 12 hours some days, taking breaks about every two hours. It was exhausting but riveting. I loved going into the city and filling the cobblestone sidewalks with music. I felt as though I contributed and became part of the fabric and charm of downtown Boston. Every day was different with an excitement of the unexpected.

After a few months on my own, away from my fiancée, Trish, I realized that our engagement just wasn't right. I wasn't truly in love. I still had no clue what love really was. We had been together for nearly six years, but our relationship hadn't deepened or developed. I broke off the engagement, and for the first time in my adult life, I felt completely free to explore the world and discover myself. I wasn't looking for a steady girlfriend, much less a wife or a fiancée. I just wanted to get through school and finish my degree.

By March of 1989, I had finished six months of co-op in Massachusetts and six more months of intense electrical-engineering courses in Cincinnati. I then moved back to Massachusetts to resume my semiconductor-engineering design work at Digital Equipment, and Brian soon started calling me again to play the piano at Lily's on evenings and weekends.

One Sunday afternoon, as I was playing that familiar baby grand at the café, a group of three girls gathered by the entrance and huddled to listen to my music. I noticed them whispering in each other's ears and pointing in my direction. One of them in particular stood out to me. She had a radiant smile—noticeable even from far across the café—and her golden hair bounced in rhythm with the liveliness of her face.

She spoke to one of the waiters and started coming toward me! I froze on the inside, but my fingers kept moving. I looked away and glanced at my set list to get my mind off her and prepare to transi-

Autumn 1990—Melissa and Robert on an afternoon date in Kansas City, Missouri

New Year's Eve 1991—Melissa and Robert's wedding reception, Cincinnati, Ohio

Photo by Sanders Photography

1993—Newlyweds on an afternoon drive from Sunnyvale to Big Sur, California

May 1997—Makenah and Robert in their new home in Liberty, Missouri

November 7, 1997—Makenah meets Zachary moments after his birth at Liberty Hospital.

1998—Melissa cherishes her special-needs son, Zachary.

June 2001—Nicholas and Zachary asleep in their Radio Flyer wagon after a long day at Rehoboth Beach, Delaware

August 2003—Bang! Nicholas guards his pizza at gunpoint.

August 13, 2003—Nicholas, Makenah, Alenah, and Zachary enjoy Popsicles on a hot summer day on their front porch—two weeks before the flash flood (this roll of film was found in the van wreckage after the flash flood).

January 2003—Home at last from China. Alenah meets her new family.

May 2003—Enjoying Memorial Day weekend along the windy Chicago waterfront

Spring 2003—Alenah's first baseball game with Daddy, Kansas City Royals Stadium

August 30, 2003—Rogers family at a relative's wedding reception in Wichita, Kansas. Last family picture ever taken

Jacob Creek's fatal flood

About 9 p.m. Saturday, heavy rain swept several motorists off I-35 south of Emporia at Jacob Creek. Extremely heavy rainfall caused the creek to overwhelm the culvert and overflow the highway, carrying with it concrete barricades and seven vehicles. Four people are confirmed dead. Two are missing.

Source: Kansas Highway Patrol, National Weather Service
Graphic and photo by Paul Soutar/The Wichita Eagle

Rescue crews searched lake for victims.

Silver minivan had been northbound. State trooper saw it being washed over the median barricade about 9 p.m. Four children are dead; their mother is missing.

Red Jeep Cherokee had been northbound. Male driver is missing.

Silver SUV: Occupants accounted for.

Silver sedan: Occupants accounted for.

Red sedan: Occupants accounted for.

Blue-green sedan: State trooper saw it being washed over the median barricade at about 9 p.m. Occupants accounted for.

Silver sedan: Occupants accounted for.

Vehicles and 10,000- to 12,000-pound concrete barriers washed off road.

Culvert normally carries Jacob Creek under highway.

Jacob Creek flows north

NORTH

Southbound lane

Northbound lane

Debris marks high-water mark on northbound lane.

August 31, 2003—The path of the Jacob Creek flash flood, I-35 milepost 116 near Emporia, Kansas

September 2003—The Rogers family minivan after rescue workers flipped it upright

September 1, 2003— After his wife's and children's bodies were recovered, Robert huddled in prayer with family members alongside the minivan wreckage.

Roadside crosses mark the flash-flood site where Robert's family perished along the Kansas Turnpike.

August 30, 2003—
Rogers children outside
the church following
the Wichita wedding
reception (this roll of
film was found in the
van wreckage after the
flash flood)

Makenah's September 2003 calendar page, drawn a year before in
autumn 2002

February 2005—Robert ministers to tsunami survivors, Andaman Islands, India.

Photo by Stephen B. Brewer

Robert begins his worldwide ministry. In 2004 alone, he gave his testimony 100 times, challenging over 21,000 people to know God and live a life of no regrets.

tion to the next song. As she approached my right side, near the tip glass, I glanced up at her glowing face. She flashed a smile I'll never forget and said, "Hey, there. You sound pretty good. What's that song you're playing?"

At that moment, I had no idea what I was playing . . . just another song. But this gorgeous lady looking at me was more than just another pretty face.

"Oh, just an old standard."

I stuttered over my words but managed to keep our conversation going. All the while I was shaking on the inside, trying to keep my fingers in tempo and on the right keys.

But as we chatted, I started to relax. She had a very pleasant and nonthreatening way about her. She was noticeably warm and kind, and yet incredibly fun and interesting. She seemed like the type of girl who never met a stranger. We kept talking and talking, and I kept playing song after song.

I learned that she grew up as a farmer's daughter in a small town called Hiawatha along the Pony Express Highway in northeastern Kansas. Shortly after she graduated from high school, she bought a one-way airline ticket to California to stay with her Uncle Bob. But at the last minute, he had called her to say that it wasn't going to work out, and she should make other plans. She then called one of her high-school friends, Kim, who was working as a nanny in Massachusetts. Kim knew of a family with three kids who needed a nanny. They interviewed her over the phone, and she got the job immediately. She switched her airline ticket to Boston and moved to the big city.

We kept talking and laughing for nearly an hour. Her friends eventually lost interest and must have left to walk around the rest of Quincy Market. I just kept right on playing the piano, and we kept right on talking. I found out that she, too, had been engaged before moving to Boston. But she had recently broken it off, partially because of the distance, but mostly because she realized the relationship wasn't the sort she wanted for marriage. She wasn't interested in a serious relationship at that time. I was relieved to hear that, because neither was I. She had just turned 19, and I had just turned 23.

When she told me she knew how to play the piano a bit, I dared her to take my spot and play a tune. She played with a very pleasant and natural style. She wasn't just playing notes. She was making music.

I felt as though we were starting to make our own music. There weren't fireworks or anything spectacular from the start. Yet something was stirring in my heart that I had never felt before.

Before she finished playing, I reached into my back pocket and pulled out my business card. I wrote my local phone number on the front and my home address in Cincinnati on the back and handed it to her.

"Here, in case you ever want to stay in touch. By the way, my name's Robert. What's yours?"

"Melissa. My name's Melissa."

"Melissa," I said aloud. Then I thought to myself, *What a beautiful name.*

"I'd better go catch up with my friends," she said.

"Okay. Thanks for sitting and talking. I hope we meet again sometime."

Then she did something I'll never forget. She reached into her purse and pulled out a five-dollar bill. She folded it up and plopped it into the tip glass. Melissa often said in later years, "That was the best five bucks I ever spent!"

But at that moment, she just tilted her head, flashed me her broad smile, gave a little wave, and left.

Melissa. Now that was an amazing lady. I didn't know her last name and had no way of getting in touch with her. But I sure hoped that she would keep in touch.

13

Ice Cream—and Love

I later learned that Melissa came back to downtown Boston that summer many times when I was at the piano. However, she never stopped to say hello. She would perch herself on a bench and just enjoy the music and write poetry.

In September, I drove back to Cincinnati to start my junior year of college. A few weeks later, I received a card in the mail from Melissa with a poem enclosed. It was one she had written over the summer while watching me from a park bench in Quincy Market. She titled it "The Piano Man."

The Piano Man
by Melissa Dawn Tollefson
early August 1989

Wherever he plays, he pleases the crowds;
Playing upbeat tunes to give the place life,
Or playing just to please our hearts,
He's always getting the attention.

And to watch his fingers dance across the keyboard,
It's a real sight to see.
For that matter, so is he.

He's always looking up to flash a smile, or just to look around,
And he'll speak with you if you stop to chat.
Ask him to play something, he'll give it a shot . . .

He's filling the air with music.
He's the piano man.

I'd never received such a poem before. It was an unexpected surprise from a girl I was secretly hoping to hear from again. It made no
mention of love, but it left the impression that I had caught her eye.

On Thanksgiving Day, the phone rang after I had finished dinner with my family at home in Cincinnati. It was for me. It was
Melissa! Our conversation flowed effortlessly, just as it had in Boston,
and lasted for nearly an hour. We talked about the importance of
family and the value of faith in God as a foundation in life. She told
me she grew up attending a small Christian church and had dedicated her life to Jesus at the age of 13.

I told her that I'd be returning to Boston in March. "Hopefully
I can see you again then."

"Yes, I'd like that," Melissa gently replied.

I was enchanted with her and couldn't wait for March to arrive
to see her again. A few days later, I bought a little card and mailed it
to her, thanking her for her poem. She told me later how she treas-
ured that simple card. After another intense semester of engineering
courses, I was ready once again to drive back to Boston to finish my

third and final co-op term. I called Melissa on that first Monday
back in Boston to wish her a happy birthday.

We made plans for me to pick her up the following Sunday. She
gave me directions to the house where she worked as a nanny, and I
arrived around lunchtime. I could barely contain my excitement.

My usual nervousness was gone. I virtually leapt up all five steps
and rang the doorbell. When she opened the door, she looked even
more bright and cheery than I had remembered. We immediately
gave each other the biggest hug, as if we had known each other all
our lives. It was odd that after only one face-to-face encounter, we
were so comfortable. Yet it felt like coming home. She looked and
smelled as fresh as the springtime air in New England. It was March
25, 1990—our first date.

We had burgers and fries at Friendly's Restaurant. As we ate, I
talked about my recent drive from Ohio to Massachusetts and about
playing the piano for some auditions earlier in the morning. We
shared easily with each other. Being around Melissa was like wearing
a shoe that fit perfectly. She just felt so natural.

After we ate, I couldn't resist the dessert menu.

"So, would you like some ice cream?"

"Yeah! Chocolate!"

She got a huge, three-dip hot-fudge sundae, and I got an overflowing peanut butter cup sundae, both made with chocolate ice
cream. I was having a blast. I could feel myself falling hard for this
beauty.

After we left Friendly's, we strolled through the park, up to a
pristine white chapel and over to an old schoolhouse nearby. We
found a gazebo farther down the road and fed some ducks there. We
enjoyed a marvelously romantic afternoon, and before we knew it,
the time had passed far too quickly.

Neither of us wanted the date to end. We gradually made it to the rental house I was living in. I took Melissa inside and introduced her to my roommates. It was now past suppertime, and we were hungry again. I offered to make us dinner.

Melissa seemed impressed that I actually knew my way around a kitchen and could cook for myself. I soon learned that one of her jobs as a nanny was to cook most of the meals for the family, and that she had been cooking for her own family since the age of 13.

After dinner, we decided to go to a movie. That night included a very special memory for both of us—our first kiss. We looked at each other afterward and burst out in laughter, as if we couldn't believe it had all happened so quickly. There was something refreshingly natural and unforced about our time together.

For the next six months, we seized every possible opportunity within reach of a day trip: whale watching in the Atlantic Ocean off the coast of Massachusetts; strolling along the rocky beaches of Kennebunkport, Maine; hiking through the White Mountains of New Hampshire; swimming and canoeing around Emerald Lake; savoring seafood at an ocean-side restaurant in Plymouth Rock near the *Mayflower*; biking around Martha's Vineyard and taking the ferry back across the channel; picnicking along the coast of Rhode Island; catching a Red Sox baseball game at Fenway Park; riding bikes along the Charles River from Cambridge into Boston; dining at romantic restaurants in Boston's North End; and catching Broadway musicals in downtown Boston and New York City.

We quickly fell deeply in love. And yet we weren't talking about long-term plans or getting married. We were just immersed in enjoying every moment at hand. We were caught up in the adventure of *now*.

Melissa trusted me with her heart . . . and with her past. She shared with me how someone she had trusted repeatedly molested her when she was a child. It had a profound and damaging effect on their relationship, but through professional counseling, she was eventually able to forgive that person and find healing. It crushed me to hear this revelation—that such a gorgeous flower of a girl had been stepped on and injured so early in life, and during such impressionable years.

After she told me this, all I could do was hold her. I couldn't conceive how someone could ever do such a horrid thing to such a beautifully innocent young girl. I was furious at whoever did this, and yet I was inspired by Melissa's amazing determination to forgive the person who had hurt her. She was truly one remarkable lady. If she could forgive, then so must I.

She confided that she was powerfully drawn to me on our first date because of my sensitive nature. It spoke volumes to her—louder than words ever could—that she could trust me. She knew that I could be gentle with her heart, which had been damaged and wounded years before.

In addition to the molestation, I learned that Melissa had been challenged by many other circumstances in her life already.

Shortly after she first arrived in Boston, she was out riding her bicycle when an automobile struck her from behind. She was thrown 30 feet through the air and landed on her right shoulder. She had little money and no health insurance, but her tenacity, determination, and faith helped her recover. Ever since then, she felt residual pain and sensitivity in her shoulder and endured it for the rest of her life.

One night not long after that accident, Melissa and a girlfriend foolishly hopped into a car with a couple of guys they didn't really know. The guys had alcohol in the trunk, and the driver was breaking traffic laws left and right. A police officer noticed their actions and stopped the car. After observing the driver, he asked everyone to get out of the car. When he inspected the trunk, he found the alcohol.

Melissa was mortified and silently prayed to God for protection. She knew she had done wrong, even though she had not taken part in any of the alcohol. And yet, rightfully so, she was still guilty by association. She and her girlfriend spent that night in jail in Hingham. The next morning she was released, and later she had to go to court. When the judge asked Melissa how old she was, she told him she was 19.

The sudden look of disappointment on his face—much like a father's—sank deep into her heart. She pled no contest to the charge of a minor in possession of alcohol and paid the fine. That one night of unwise choices, and of God's protecting grace over her life, taught her many lessons. She realized how truly naive she still was at 19 and that she wasn't as invincible as she felt. From then on, she made much wiser choices in life.

Growing up on a farm, she had sustained a number of injuries. Over the years, barbed wire fences, knives, and meat hooks had inflicted deep slits in her arms and legs. Plus, as a result of cheerleading and basketball injuries, she suffered torn ligaments and wore out the meniscus in her right knee, requiring three corrective arthroscopic surgeries.

On top of all that, their family farm went bankrupt while she was in high school, and her parents divorced shortly after the bankruptcy. With the added instability at home, Melissa rebelled with the wrong crowd in high school and did things she later regretted. She was dating a guy who lived several hours away, and around the age of 17 she became engaged to him.

While driving home alone from his house late one night, she fell asleep at the wheel of her Thunderbird. It screeched sideways on the highway, and Melissa awoke suddenly, grabbing the steering wheel. All four tires ripped off the rims, and the Thunderbird careened off the road, down the embankment, and into a ditch. Melissa was wearing her seat belt and miraculously escaped injury. Even then, God was watching over her. Melissa often said of those tenuous times, "God smiles on my ignorance."

From all the wounds Melissa had already endured at such a young age, she seemed to find great comfort and solace in my arms. I was eager to introduce her to the rest of my family.

That opportunity would come at Easter.

14

Dreams and Heartaches

Any fears I had that Melissa wouldn't connect with my parents evaporated from the moment they met at my brother John's house in Connecticut on Easter weekend. Melissa and my father bonded instantly, chatting over in a corner for more than an hour.

The summer flew by. Melissa left for Seattle, where she was planning to start college, and I returned to Cincinnati to finish my degree in electrical engineering. But when classes resumed, all I could think of was Melissa. I called her every day, but our calls never seemed long enough. I knew I loved her, but I hadn't even seriously considered proposing to her until now—now that we were apart.

A few weeks into my senior year, my close friend Janet came to Cincinnati for a short visit. She was about to marry a wonderful gentleman named Kirk. Their wedding was set for October—just a few weeks away—and I was going to play the piano for the ceremony. While we were discussing music, I told her all about Melissa. Talking about Melissa and sharing the stories of all the fun we'd had together, it hit me how much she meant to me.

For the first time in my life, I understood what true love was. I wanted to marry this girl.

Only God could have taken a city boy from Cincinnati and a country girl from Kansas and crossed our paths in the middle of downtown Boston. This revelation made my college switch from music to engineering all worthwhile. God had used it all for good, as He promised in His Word (Romans 8:28).

When I received the phone bill for our first month of calls between Cincinnati and Seattle, it was more than three hundred dollars! Not long after that, Melissa called me one night with a question: "I want to drop out of school and come to be with you. Will you have me?"

I was thrilled, but I paused for a moment and thought to myself, *If I say yes, then I'm committing right now in my heart to marry her. I'm not going to say yes and then drop her anytime soon—not after she quits college and drives clear across the country just to be with me.*

"Yes," I answered firmly. "Come on out to Cincinnati, Melissa."

She shouted gleefully at the top of her lungs and started packing as soon as we hung up. The moment I saw her Thunderbird pull into the driveway on Locust Lane, I bolted down the stairs, flung open the door, and opened my arms wide to greet her. It was reminiscent of our first hug on the porch steps back in March in Massachusetts. It felt like coming home again.

I was certain that she was the one for me. She quickly found an apartment for herself and a job as a waitress. For the next two and a half months, Melissa never even hinted at getting married or engaged. I sneaked out to a jeweler and chose an engagement ring and wedding band.

On Christmas Eve, we attended midnight Mass at St. Xavier Catholic Church with my parents. Afterward, Melissa and I drove to Kansas to spend Christmas Day with her family.

A couple of days later, I was able to have a moment alone with

Liz, Melissa's mother, at the farmer's co-op in Hiawatha where she worked.

I was honest with her about my strong feelings for Melissa. "Liz, I think the world of Melissa, and I love her. I'd like to ask for your daughter's hand in marriage."

She instantly responded, "Well, all right! I thought I'd never get her hitched!" That made us both laugh.

Melissa and I drove back to Cincinnati for New Year's Eve. I had made reservations for us to attend a dinner-dance cruise on the Ohio River on BB Riverboats. Melissa's wavy golden hair looked stunning against her black blazer. After our meal, I got up from our table near the windows and led her over to the upright piano on the dance floor.

Weeks in advance, I had scoped out the boat and cleared my plans with the captain. I pulled up a chair next to the piano and invited Melissa to sit, facing me. I sat down at the piano bench and started playing one of the first songs I had ever played for her at Lily's Sidewalk Café in Boston: "Your Song" by Elton John. About halfway through the song, the captain of the ship—knowing full well what I had concocted—brought over a microphone on a boom stand and shoved it in front of my mouth so the entire boat could hear me. By now, the dinner conversation had quieted down and everyone was watching me. I added a tag to the ending of the song and sang my own words to the chorus:

How wonderful life would be
If you would marry me . . .

Melissa's jaw dropped, and she covered her mouth with both hands. Tears welled up in her eyes. Everyone who had heard me propose over the speakers throughout the ship went "Awwwww . . ."

in unison. I got down onto one knee, reached into my pocket, and pulled out the sparkling engagement ring.

"Melissa, will you marry me?"

She was now crying and could only squeeze out indecipherable pops and squeaks. I couldn't tell for sure what she was trying to say. I gave her a few moments, and with no clear answer in sight, I inquired, "Well . . . ?"

Finally, she was able to collect her breath and say, "Yes. Yes! *YES!*" Everyone on the ship erupted into spontaneous applause. With my hands shaking from nervous apprehension and her hands shaking from sheer jubilation, I somehow managed to place the ring on her finger. We stood up, embraced, and kissed for all to see. Then we danced away the rest of the night into the new year—1991—in love and engaged to be married.

We set our wedding date for New Year's Eve 1991. That gave us one year to plan and pay for our wedding. Digital Equipment, where I had done my co-op work, offered me a job. But neither Melissa nor I felt certain about putting down roots in the northeast. I accepted another offer from S-MOS Systems in San Jose, in the heart of Silicon Valley.

There was an allure about California to me, an aura of adventure and charm that I had always wanted to experience. Melissa felt the same way. I was to start work there in September, so after graduation, I played in a wedding reception band for the rest of the summer while Melissa found a new job at Circuit City. We had a blast making our wedding plans together—choosing the cake, the flowers, the Victorian mansion reception hall, the tables and chairs, the tablecloths, the invitations, the caterer, the DJ, the limo, the floating-candle centerpieces, and all the other sundry details.

About halfway through the summer, however, Melissa started

acting strangely. It seemed as if she was distancing herself from me. I still loved her deeply, but it felt as though we were growing apart. She wasn't as loving and affectionate as usual. I finally confronted her about her mood.

"Melissa, are you okay? Is everything all right? Have I done or said anything wrong to hurt you?"

She started crying and admitted through her tears that she had become friends with a guy at work. They had taken a walk during a lunch break recently, and he had kissed her. She confessed that she had some feelings for him. I couldn't believe what I was hearing. It tore my heart out.

"Give me back the ring," I said, holding out my hand.

Through her tears and her long hair, dangling in her face now, she reluctantly relinquished it. I couldn't remain engaged to someone who wasn't 100 percent committed and devoted to us as a couple.

"Melissa, I don't get this. I don't understand. I love you, and I want to marry you, but not if you can't make up your mind . . . not if you don't believe in us!"

As she cried, she grew hysterical and on the verge of hyperventilating. Her hands were shaking, and she was having trouble standing. I had to hold her in my arms just to keep her from collapsing.

"I know, Robert," she sobbed. "I'm sorry. I'm so sorry. I love you, too. I really do. I'm just . . . I'm just so sorry."

It was clear that there was more to this than just another guy. It struck me as a rebellion toward our relationship, as if she was trying to sabotage it or something. I knew I had to dig deeper.

I held her for nearly an hour to calm her down. Her breathing finally returned to normal, and I took her back to her apartment. During the half-hour drive to my home, I kept trying to sort through all the details and questions in my mind. It seemed to me that Melissa was still carrying around a great deal of inward pain and distrust.

Because she had been molested by someone she had trusted, she obviously wasn't sure if she could count on my love and my trust for a lifetime. Because she was wounded, it was difficult for her to accept that she could fully receive unconditional love. I wondered if she had to run away like a prodigal, only to return home where she always knew she belonged. I think she wanted to hurt our relationship before it could hurt her.

Because of my faith upbringing, and from seeing the example of my parents forgiving each other countless times, I knew I had to forgive Melissa, despite the hurt I was feeling. But could we make it past this? Could I trust her again?

15

From Forgiveness to Forever

Melissa's fling and the result of that was a critical moment for the fabric of our relationship. I had two clear choices: I could continue to love Melissa through this—forgive her and show her that she could indeed trust me not to leave or hurt her, or I could say good-bye for good to the girl I had fallen in love with and leave her in a perpetual state of mistrust and rejection. If I had left her, she may never have trusted anyone again.

I chose to love and forgive. It hurt deeply, but to me it was the only choice. I truly loved Melissa and still wanted to marry her. It was the first true test of our love and commitment and was terribly painful at times. It taught me that pain is often the price you pay for love. It tested my faith and dared me to depend solely on God's love, because human love can fail and betray you.

Over time, I also realized that the effects of childhood molestation would surface sporadically throughout the rest of Melissa's life. There were many offshoots, flashbacks, and related events. Throughout our marriage, she would occasionally shut down and curl up in a ball, shivering, rocking, and gasping for air. If I tried to touch her, she would often flinch and lash out. Eventually, she would allow me to enter her personal space and let me hold her, silently rocking back and forth. She also suffered from feelings of insecurity and low self-esteem.

Forgiveness is such a powerful thing. When I forgave Melissa, it set us both free. It set Melissa free from guilt and condemnation. It set me free from bitterness and grudges that could have lasted a lifetime.

A few weeks later, I proposed to Melissa again next to the Ohio River, and we resumed our wedding plans. In mid-September, I moved out to California. Within a few days, I had found a nice two-bedroom apartment in Sunnyvale. While I was gone, Melissa finalized our wedding plans and continued saving money.

Finally, December arrived. I flew the red-eye on Christmas Eve from San Francisco through New York City to Cincinnati. We lifted off the runway around 11:00 P.M. A few hours later, I met Melissa at the airport in Cincinnati. We couldn't believe we were finally here. From the blissful months of courtship in New England to the agonizing moments of uncertainty, our relationship had been tested with fire and proved to be the right stuff—the real thing that good marriages are made of.

Before I knew it, our wedding day—New Year's Eve 1991—was upon us. I made it to the church on time and noticed that the white limo was already out front. That could only mean one thing: Melissa and her bridesmaids had already arrived!

I hadn't seen Melissa all day. When the processional finally began, the bridesmaids and groomsmen each carried a candle to light the way. Saint Lawrence church was aglow inside with Christmas lights and poinsettias. A cream-colored tulle fabric lined both sides of the aisle as Jenna, our flower girl, dropped dried rose petals from all the flowers I had given Melissa over the past 12 months.

But all the beauty of the sanctuary paled in comparison to Melissa when the magnificent doors opened at the end of the aisle. She was stunning. She savored the long, slow walk down the aisle, escorted by her mother on her left and her father on her right.

Her long golden hair was French-braided from each side and met in the back to form one braid. Her veil tucked into her hair at the top of the braid. Her dress was made out of candlelight ivory satin overlaid with white lace accents, giving it a classic antique look. The crown centerpiece of her dress was her grandmother's antique cameo heirloom. She wore the cameo on a plain satin ribbon as a choker.

Melissa and I professed our love for each other, reciting our wedding vows from memory.

Before we walked into our reception, I pulled her close and kissed her under the doorway. Almost in unison, we both exclaimed, "We did it!" We burst into the front room to cheers and music. We quickly dove into dinner, cut the scrumptious white-chocolate wedding cake—complete with ice cream and strawberries on the side—and danced until the clock rang in 1992. It was a magical night to begin the New Year and our new lives together.

We enjoyed a fun-filled honeymoon week: three days at Disney World in Florida, and four days on a Caribbean cruise. After our honeymoon, we drove more than 2,500 miles to California.

I pulled off Highway 101 onto Fair Oaks Avenue in Sunnyvale and into our apartment complex. I ran upstairs and unlocked the door, ran back down, and carried Melissa all the way to our new abode, across the threshold. We made it! We did it! We were finally married and living in California.

16

Makenah Arrives

As we settled into our apartment in Sunnyvale, we began whit-
tling away at the mountain of debt built from our wedding,
honeymoon, and school and car loans.

We were determined to pay off our debt quickly, but we were
also determined to tithe. Years before, I had learned from Scripture
the principle of tithing—giving 10 percent of all our income to God.
To us, tithing was an expression of honor and worship to God. It was
thanksgiving for all He blessed us with. With the high cost of living
in Silicon Valley, tithing really stretched our faith, even though
Melissa and I both had jobs. Some months it was not easy to make
ends meet.

To our delight, we discovered that we couldn't outgive God. He
was faithful, met our needs, and blessed us as His Word promised.
Within two years, we had paid off the $25,000 in debts we had accu-
mulated. It felt so good. Instead of pocketing the "extra" money, we
kept making monthly car and loan payments—only this time, we
paid ourselves. We put it into savings so that we could buy a home
someday.

Throughout our marriage, I sensed that Melissa needed the reassurance of knowing that I loved her unconditionally, and that it was okay for her to trust me. Because her trust was shattered during childhood, it took years to rebuild. I was laying bricks with every little "I love you" and every little note I wrote her, reinforcing a basic yet profound theme: "I love you with my life, Melissa."

We started having a "Love Lunch" once a month. I would find a place around Silicon Valley that we hadn't visited before and meet Melissa there for lunch. It didn't have to be fancy, but those little love lunches became very special to us.

We also learned the value of taking daily walks together. Adapting to each other in a new environment with no family or friends nearby was an enormous adjustment for us. Melissa and I had to learn to live with each other and blend our quirky habits. The walks gave us time alone to talk things through, to dream aloud about the future, and to discuss topics like having children.

Yet I made a big mistake our first year of marriage. I became overinvolved in music at our church, Jubilee Christian Center. I volunteered to play piano for the Tongues of Fire Choir, for the junior high group, for the Saturday night service, and on the road for our music pastor. All of those commitments took me away from Melissa so much that it detracted from our marriage. It was as if I was having an affair with music. One night, I was recording a song for Pastor Ron Kenoly at his home, and I asked his advice about what I should do.

"Robert, family is your first ministry," he told me.

Pastor Ron's words struck home. How could I worship God on the piano while my marriage was falling apart at home? I immediately made adjustments to focus my time and energies on our family, although it was painful to resign from ministries I loved. But I needed to be a husband to Melissa first and show her my consistent love and commitment. I'm thankful I learned this valuable lesson before we started having children. I realized that it's entirely possible to be busy doing right things, and still not do things right. My priority needed to be my family.

As we approached our third year of marriage, Melissa and I were growing more and more anxious to have children. We both wanted a big family. However, month after month came and went, and we still weren't pregnant. Our family physician said to wait a full year before trying alternatives. Her advice to us both was to just relax.

Melissa stopped working at Circuit City and enrolled in her second year as a full-time student in interior design at West Valley College in August 1994. The doctor's advice worked. In early December Melissa learned that she was pregnant. When I got home that same night, Melissa told me I had an early Christmas present hidden in our tree—it was the home-pregnancy test result. She turned up the stereo so I could hear the song playing in the background: "Unborn Heart" by Dan Hill. As I listened to the first line about having a baby and put that together with the explosive excitement in Melissa's face, it hit me. We were going to have a baby!

I did my best to indulge Melissa's cravings for crackers, pickles, hominy, pork and beans, noodle soup, toasted peanut-butter-and-jelly, and bagels with cream cheese. I also talked to our baby every day, putting my mouth to Melissa's tummy and saying how much we loved and were praying for our baby. That Christmas was wonderfully memorable as we shared the news in person with family back home. As a gift to our baby, Melissa and I started a journal together, chronicling our feelings and experiences from conception through birth of what it felt like as first-time parents to experience this new life growing inside Melissa.

One of Melissa's journal entries in the first trimester proved to be prophetic:

> *January 24, 1995*
> *Oh, Baby! I'm in my second day of school. It's hectic already. I can feel you growing inside of me. Yesterday, I woke up feeling SO pregnant! This Friday your Daddy and I heard your heartbeat for the first time. . . . You waved at me and kicked a lot, then you waved again. It gave me chills, Baby. You are our little Miracle. We have lots of people praying for us. We want you to be in perfect health. . . . Baby—you're gonna be a world-shaker and a history-maker. We love you bunches.*

Melissa carried our baby like a watermelon—all out in front. She developed the cutest little waddle when she walked. I loved showing her off to people at church or at the grocery store. We attended Bradley childbirth classes and learned a lot about home birth. In particular, we liked the idea of water birth because of all the benefits for the mother and baby—assuming everything goes smoothly during the birth process. We selected a nearby midwife with whom we felt comfortable and decided on an at-home water birth.

None of our parents were crazy about the idea of a home birth—including Melissa's mom, who had had a difficult time delivering Robbie, Melissa's brother. Still, with the hospital only 10 minutes away, and our friend KK—a registered nurse—less than five minutes away, we felt fine about giving birth at home.

But our baby had other plans.

Melissa's mother came out to California for a week in early August, hoping to be present at the birth. But Melissa didn't go into labor until August 11, the day after her mother left. My mother arrived from Cincinnati, and we were all so excited that we were going to have our baby that day. I moved the dining room table to the side of the room and inflated the small six-foot pool we had rented for a water birth. But after 24 hours of hard labor, Melissa still wasn't dilated nearly enough to deliver our baby. We were both discouraged, and she was utterly exhausted.

For eight months, we had prayed repeatedly for a smooth, short delivery. Why wasn't God answering our prayers? We were so frustrated. I stayed right at Melissa's side, rubbing her shoulders, massaging her feet, and pressing her lower back during contractions. I wanted to be with her for every moment of this.

More hours passed.

Finally, after 36 hours of labor, our midwife told us that Melissa needed to go to the hospital. We couldn't believe how difficult this labor was. It was the most traumatic and excruciating ordeal we had experienced together.

After 48 full hours of intense labor, Dr. Hoff, one of two doctors (who were also brothers) assisting us, said, "Melissa, it's dangerous for you and your baby now. You've given it your best shot. There aren't many options left. We're going to have to deliver by C-section."

Our hearts sank. We wanted a smooth, at-home water birth, not an invasive C-section surgery with incisions, sutures, drugs, and IVs. Deep down, I was disappointed with God.

I sat next to Melissa's head, behind the operating screen. The operation went smoothly, although Melissa could feel the doctors working inside of her because the epidural numbed only one side of her body. I asked everyone there not to announce whether our baby was a boy or girl. We agreed that I would announce it as a surprise.

We had already picked out a boy name and a girl name. So one of the Hoff brothers kept saying, "I see it. I see it! It's aaaaaaaaa . . . bbbbbbbb . . . baby! Yup. It's definitely a baby!" We all flinched as he nearly blew the long-anticipated surprise. "I didn't say it. I didn't say it!" he chimed back.

During the operation, the doctors kept teasing us over and over, pretending to almost reveal the big secret that everyone was eagerly awaiting.

Finally, at 9:04 P.M., they said, "Oh, look at that!! What a beautiful baby!" They lifted her up, and my eyes filled with tears. I gazed at our firstborn child and said to Melissa, "It's . . . Makenah!" I hugged Melissa, and we cried together, "We have a little girl!"

I was so excited. They cleaned Makenah and weighed her. She came in at a whopping 9 pounds, 11 ounces, and 22 inches long. She had great color and muscle tone, long fingers, and huge feet—three and a half inches long! She had the cutest strawberry-blond hair and a little strawberry birthmark on the nape of her neck. We didn't know it until then, but she was sunny-side up—facing up instead of down. She was stuck in the birth canal and came out with a cone head from all of Melissa's pushing.

The doctors said there was no way Makenah would have been able to come out the birth canal normally in that position at that size. My initial disappointment with the situation turned into thankfulness to God for His provision. If we had not come to the hospital, Melissa would not have been able to safely give birth. I recognized that God had been with us through the entire excruciating birth process.

They placed Makenah in my arms, and I gently held her close, like a fine piece of china. Daddy's little girl . . . my first daughter. I wanted to treat her with such kid gloves. I didn't want to break her. I brought her close to Melissa's head as she lay there, still in pain as the doctors worked. Even after this endless ordeal, Melissa's weary face lit up at the sight of Makenah as she declared, "She was worth it!" I comforted Makenah as I sang the "Psalm 139 Lullaby" I had written for her.

In a moment, all the agony and despair of the past two days melted away. God had replaced it with indescribable joy. Through all 48 hours of pain that Melissa had endured, God saw fit to bring a mighty blessing.

We learned a valuable lesson: Even though everything that happens to us is not always good, God can still bring good out of everything. Makenah's difficult delivery was an experience that ultimately took us deeper in our faith.

17

A Brush with Death

The next year offered numerous firsts: Makenah's first trip home in the car, her first bath, her first trip to church, her first smile, and on and on. Our baby turned one on August 13, 1996. About the time we began weaning Makenah, Melissa flew up to Seattle with her over the weekend to visit her Uncle John, who was nearly 98 years old. They flew home on Monday night. Because I missed both of my girls terribly, I decided to stay home from work Tuesday morning.

That morning, we took our time waking up and getting ready. All three of us just relaxed in our bed and lingered awhile. We needed some groceries, so I packed the diaper bag and bottle after breakfast.

"Melissa, are you ready?" I hollered up the stairs. "I just changed Makenah's diaper. She's in the carrier, and we're all set to go."

I heard a faint voice from our bedroom at the top of the stairs. "Robert, you better come up here."

I ran upstairs and saw Melissa sprawled out on our bed on her back, white as a sheet. "I don't feel so well." I felt her forehead and face. She was cold, pale, and clammy.

"I feel so weak." Melissa sounded more and more faint with every word that came out of her mouth. I called El Camino Hospital immediately and explained Melissa's symptoms. "Get her down here right away!" the nurse commanded.

I slammed down the phone, carried Melissa's limp body down the steps and out the door, and placed her into the passenger seat. I buckled her seat belt, ran inside, and grabbed Makenah in her carrier along with the diaper bag and bottle. With Makenah secure in the backseat, I raced to El Camino Hospital 10 minutes away. Along the way, Melissa was virtually delirious, moaning and groaning. Then she said something that sent shivers down my spine.

"I can't see."

"What do you mean, you can't see?"

"All I can see is white!"

Inside, I was freaking out. *She's dying!* I prayed aloud in the car for God's protection.

When I reached the hospital, I ran in, gave our name, and grabbed a wheelchair. A nurse ran back out with me and helped slide Melissa's slumped body into the wheelchair. "Take good care of her," I pleaded as the nurse wheeled her in.

I parked the car and grabbed Makenah and the diaper bag. I was so thankful for Makenah. Her peaceful demeanor throughout the whole ordeal helped give me peace. I checked in at the admitting desk, filled out some forms, and gave our insurance cards to the receptionist.

After all the paperwork, they led me to an emergency room where I found Melissa on her back. She looked terrible. They had already hooked up an IV to give her fluids, and a phlebotomist was trying to draw blood from her arm.

"Do you know what's happening?" I asked.

"Not yet," he said as he worked.

He wasn't getting any blood. He poked her arm again and again. Still, nothing.

"I'm sorry, ma'am. I have to keep trying until I get blood."

Melissa was moaning, as if she were talking in her sleep. "That's okay. I don't care. Just do whatever you need to," she mumbled.

The phlebotomist was eventually able to draw a few drops of blood.

"Her blood pressure is terribly low," he said, concern in his voice.

"What could it be? What's going on?" I pleaded.

"We'll find out right away."

He took the partially full vial of blood out of the room to run tests.

I called our parents to let them know what was happening and to ask them to pray for us. I kept talking to Melissa, whether or not she responded, just trying to keep her conscious and lucid. Nearly an hour passed, and I was terribly worried that she would die while they were trying to figure out what was wrong. Finally, someone hurried into the ER and said, "We've got to take her into emergency surgery."

"Now?" I asked.

"Right now!"

"Why?"

"She's pregnant and likely just had an ectopic rupture. She's bleeding internally. She could die."

She could die? God, help us!

As I stood there shell-shocked, they whisked Melissa away and directed me to the waiting room. We were going to have another baby? We had no idea.

God, this doesn't make any sense! I prayed silently. *Why? We prayed for a large family. We prayed for healthy children. We've done our best to remain faithful and obedient. We're on Your side, here! How could You let this happen?*

I had always believed that God is good and that He has only good things in store for us. But this incident shook my faith to its core. I was disappointed that, once again, we encountered a major detour in life. Things didn't go anywhere near the way we had planned.

Then it hit me: *What if I had gone to work today? What if I hadn't stayed home?* Melissa would have died lying on our bed, unable to reach our phone. Makenah could have been crying in her crib or on the floor all day. I recognized the hand of Providence that had prompted me to stay home that morning so that I could be there for Melissa at just the right time.

Again I realized that God's plans may not be our plans, but He's always right on time. I had to accept the reality that attending church faithfully, tithing, and putting God first in our marriage did not ensure that we would never experience trials or heartache. We *were* promised, however, that God would never leave us or forsake us. I had to surrender my anger, my disappointment, and my bitterness toward God for allowing this to happen to my wife and second child. Bitterness and anger would only fester and grow inside. I had to accept His will and His purpose.

I clutched Makenah a little closer as I felt such a sobering and somber brush with death twice in one day: Melissa and our second baby. Life felt terribly fragile. It was so easy—especially in a materialistic environment like Silicon Valley—to become comfortable and complacent in our little world. This day reminded me that *everything* could change in the blink of an eye.

Hours later, the surgeon emerged from the doorway, looking as though he had just finished a mile relay.

"She's going to be okay," he told me. "She would have died if you hadn't brought her here in time. She lost a lot of blood into her abdomen—nearly 80 percent. We were able to give her back some of her own after we filtered it, but we had to give her several transfusions, too."

"What happened?"

"Did you know she was pregnant?"

"No, we didn't. We thought as long as Melissa was nursing, our chances of getting pregnant were slim."

"Well, she was pregnant, and the baby lodged in one of her tubes. The tube burst and she bled internally. She lost her tube, but I was able to save her ovary."

Despite these complications, the doctor assured us that we could still have children.

While I was relieved that Melissa had survived, I still reeled at the enormity of what had happened.

Melissa recovered quickly. Since we believed our baby's soul lives forever—that a person is a person, no matter how small—we named our child Baby Hope. We were hopeful for the day we would meet in heaven, and we were hopeful we would conceive another child.

Once again, God was faithful. As Makenah was just learning to speak, one of her first words was "baby." She kept saying it over and over again: "Baby . . . baby . . . baby." Her words turned out to be prophetic. Within half a year, we were expecting our next baby!

We were also anticipating moving away from California and closer to family. After more than five years, we had had enough of the West Coast and throwing away money on rent. We had never made enough money to afford a down payment on a house, and we had a deep desire to buy our own home and put down roots somewhere in the Midwest. We decided on Kansas City—by Melissa's family. She wanted to rebuild relationships with her two brothers and her parents. Her dad had recently remarried, and Melissa wanted to get to know her new stepmother. We truly felt "called" to Kansas City.

Kansas City wasn't a hotbed of technology like Silicon Valley. I searched the paper and the Internet, sent out résumés, and used a "headhunter" to find an engineering job. Maxon Electronics, near Kansas City International Airport, flew us out to interview over Valentine's Day weekend in 1997. The initial interview went superbly, and we arranged to go house hunting with a real estate agent on Saturday. She lined up five homes around the metro area in order to get an idea of our tastes. She honestly didn't expect us to latch on to any of them. But then we set eyes on the fifth home in Liberty, Missouri: a one-and-a-half-story Cape Cod home with about 2,600 square feet and more than an acre of land, all at an incredible price. Virtually in unison, we said, "This is a great place to raise a family."

The home had just gone on the market that Friday, and we were the first ones to see it on Saturday. The next day, I sent an earnest deposit check in the mail to hold it. We closed the sale from California and rented a 24-foot Ryder truck to move all our belongings. Melissa was two months pregnant, and Makenah was over a year and a half old. She kept learning new words and started saying "Boy . . . boy . . . boy" over and over. Since she was right about another "baby," we wondered if she was right about a "boy," too.

After we arrived in Liberty, Melissa's family helped us unpack all in one afternoon. We stocked the pantry and connected the washer and dryer on the first day. Instantly, it felt like home. We finally owned our own house. God was so faithful and good to us, once again.

18

What's Going On, God?

The next seven months flew by. When Melissa's due date came and went, we decided to take no chances: We scheduled the baby's delivery to be induced on November 6, 1997.

Melissa had some contractions, but nothing abnormal or as intense as the last time. After we calmly checked into the hospital around 5:00 P.M., the doctor examined Melissa and determined that she was already in labor and dilated to five centimeters. She wouldn't have to be induced after all. God was answering our prayers! Without even realizing it, Melissa had already dilated as far as she had after 48 long hours with Makenah.

"This should be a breeze, compared to Makenah's birth!" Melissa exclaimed.

We walked the hallways and stretched as we had learned in childbirth classes. Melissa had intense contractions for nine solid hours. Thankfully, they were productive. At 2:01 A.M. on November 7, after lots of forceful pushing, and in a huge scream and burst of pain, Melissa gave birth to our firstborn son!

"It's a . . . boy! You did it, bubby, you did it!" I exclaimed, as I saw him being born. We were so thrilled to have a son.

We intentionally waited again until the birth to discover whether we had a boy or a girl. During each pregnancy, we signed a doctor's waiver to refuse the amniocentesis. We really didn't see the point. The test itself involved a risk of miscarriage. Plus, it would only indicate the gender and any abnormalities. None of that mattered to us. We were going to accept whatever child God blessed us with. Our son was beautiful—all 8 pounds, 1 ounce, and 21 inches of him. He had lots of blond hair and looked like a mix between Melissa's dad and my Grandpa Meyer. But as they cleaned him up, he wasn't making much noise.

"Is everything okay?" I asked as I held Melissa's hand and stroked her hair.

They assured me that all was well.

"Way to go, Melissa. You did it!" I congratulated her for such incredible determination and resolve to give birth naturally without painkillers.

They brought our son over to Melissa, and she snuggled him close in her arms. We hadn't settled on a name yet. We had several names ready, but we wanted to hold him first to see which one fit best.

We were mesmerized. He was absolutely beautiful. I felt so proud to have a handsome son. Wow, we had a boy and a girl now! God was so good to us! We looked at each other and unanimously said, "Zachary?" Yes, Zachary. His name was Zachary Seth. It meant "appointed and placed by God." We sensed already that he was indeed hand-placed by God in our lives. There was something very special about him.

Grandma Liz brought Makenah in from the waiting room to greet her new brother. "Makenah, look! You have a new little brother named Zachary!" She was half asleep and half in shock. She just stared at him and smiled.

Over the next 24 hours, Zachary got lots of attention. Nurses kept taking him for special tests and X-rays. He hadn't yet dirtied a diaper, and they were concerned. Finally, they were about to wheel him out again when I asked, "What's going on? Why are you taking so many X-rays of him?"

Surprised, the nurse asked, "Well, didn't they tell you?"

"Tell us what?"

She raised her eyebrows and obviously stopped short of saying something. She grappled a bit for the right words, and then just settled for, "I better get the doctor."

Melissa and I looked at each other—puzzled and bewildered—wondering what could possibly be the problem. Zachary looked perfectly angelic to us. His vitals were good, and he was eating well.

Dr. Stephanie Marx, his pediatrician, entered the room with a somber, slightly forced smile on her face. "Why don't you both sit down?"

Melissa and I listened in disbelief when Dr. Marx said, "Mr. and Mrs. Rogers, we believe your son has Down syndrome."

Melissa and I were so shocked we couldn't speak.

Dr. Marx kept talking, but I didn't comprehend another word she said. I felt as though somebody had just hit me in the gut with a baseball bat. Questions raced through my mind: *What? Down syndrome? What exactly is that—a temporary disease or a permanent condition? Will he get better? Will it eventually go away? Will he grow out of it? How could that happen? What does this mean?*

After several minutes of explanation, Dr. Marx got up to leave and indicated that Zachary needed to go by ambulance to Children's Mercy Hospital in downtown Kansas City right away for heart and bowel complications. She left the room, and all Melissa and I could do was hold each other in stunned disbelief and cry in each other's arms. A few hours earlier, we were still euphoric from Zachary's smooth labor and delivery. Now, with two simple words of enormous implication—Down syndrome—all of that euphoria was replaced by a cloud of heavy doubt and disbelief.

We met the ambulance crew in another room. Zachary was secured in an incubator-type enclosure. I couldn't touch or hold my own son. I felt as if I had completely lost control of the situation.

A very kind Catholic priest from our local St. James parish was the chaplain on duty at the hospital. He joined us in the room and led us in prayer as they loaded Zachary into the ambulance. We were supposed to be heading home now with Zachary in the backseat, just like we did after Makenah's birth. Instead, we had to follow this ambulance carrying our son to Children's Mercy, a hospital we had never been to before and knew nothing about.

As we pulled onto I-35, I started praying aloud: "Dear God, in Jesus' name, I ask that You heal our son. Take care of him and fix this Down syndrome right away—whatever the cause is—just as we prayed that he would be perfectly healthy and whole. Lord, what's going on? What's happening? How could You let this happen to our son? This doesn't make sense! *God, I don't understand! Why, God? Why?*"

My prayer deteriorated to a one-sided yelling match. Tears were streaming down my cheeks. I lost it. I was yelling at God. I was angry with God. I was disappointed. I was confused. I didn't understand. It seemed as though God had let me down again and that He didn't love us. He had allowed our son to be stricken with something that was apparently incurable.

Melissa was crying profusely too. As I sobbed and drove, she bubbled forth in prayers of healing for our son. We parked in the garage and followed the signs to the admissions desk, still stunned in disbelief that we had to be there. The kind lady behind the desk asked for insurance cards and gave us a form to fill out. As I scribbled in the blanks, I felt like telling her, "No, you don't understand. There's been a mistake. You see, we prayed that our son would be fine, so we're not really supposed to be here. They obviously have our son confused with someone else."

I later found out that this facility was actually one of the best children's hospitals in the nation—a Kansas City amenity for which we became extremely grateful. We made our way to the neonatal intensive-care unit (NICU) and found this little "cubicle" dedicated to the care of Zachary. Next to a rocking chair lay our son. He was tucked behind a clear plastic enclosure, attached to myriad wires and tubes. My heart sank as I saw him in this helpless environment. It felt as if we had taken 50 steps backward. All I wanted to do was grab him and whisk him home—away from all of this.

We gradually learned more about Down syndrome. A genetic counselor explained that Zachary was still a baby first and encouraged us not to call him a "Down's baby" but instead a "baby with Down syndrome." The Down syndrome was secondary. She emphasized that we should treat our son like any other child, even with his special needs. High expectations would help him function better. Thankfully, Zachary had fairly good muscle tone, which would benefit his gross motor skills and overall development.

We learned that Down syndrome is a genetic chromosomal disorder that occurs once in every 900 births. It is not inherited. It's a fluke. Genetic tests concluded that Zachary was born with "trisomy 21," the most common form of Down syndrome. Instead of the normal two chromosomes, the 21st set forms with three. Every cell in Zachary's body had this extra chromosome. From the moment of birth, the doctors were certain of the diagnosis, based on his features:

his slanted eyes, his small ears, the flat bridge of his nose, and so on. In fact, we later discovered that the entire birthing team recognized it right away but respectfully didn't share their suspicions with us.

Since it was a fluke, I couldn't help but wonder *Why?* and *What if?* Only God knew the answers. Once we overcame the shock of Zachary's condition, we had to release our expectations and move forward. We had chosen not to have the amniocentesis because we had said we would accept whatever child God gave us. Now we had to live up to those words and truly accept the child He had given us.

I didn't know why Zachary was born with Down syndrome, but I did learn one thing for certain: Zachary was divinely placed in our lives. We had a deep sense that God was going to use Zachary to reach out and draw others to His heart somehow. Later, in church, we were encouraged by the story of Jesus healing the blind man:

> As [Jesus] went along, he saw a man blind from birth. His disciples asked him, "Rabbi, who sinned, this man or his parents, that he was born blind?"
>
> "Neither this man nor his parents sinned," said Jesus, "but this happened so that the work of God might be displayed in his life." (John 9:1–3)

That Scripture passage told the story of a man who was randomly stricken with a condition since birth, much like Zachary. It showed people asking why it happened—much like us—and Jesus assuring them that it was not a punishment for anyone's sins, just as Down syndrome isn't anyone's fault. And most importantly, it showed how God used a genetic condition for good to display His power.

We prayed the same would happen through Zachary's life. During those first two weeks and then over the course of his remaining years, we drastically adjusted our lives and never relented to an onslaught of complications: surgeries to correct intestinal issues and hernias, frequent pneumonia from aspirating fluid into his lungs, crossed eyes, flat feet, and other physical challenges.

Not only did Zachary meet the state criteria for a child with mental retardation, he was also autistic. He had a receptive and expressive language disorder and very low attentiveness. His hearing was fine, but his communication was severely impaired. We learned sign language as a family to communicate with him. He maintained minimal eye contact, couldn't articulate, and needed help engaging in conversation. He needed encouragement to initiate peer play, creative play, and appropriate play with toys. He grew frustrated when he wasn't included, and it seemed to hurt his feelings. He thrived on routine, habit, and repetition in familiar surroundings.

He got frustrated if anyone deviated from the norm even a little. When frustrated, he sometimes banged his head against a wall, once to the point of damaging the drywall. When tired, he would sit and slowly rock himself, making clicking noises with his tongue. With the proper encouragement, he would participate in class routines like circle time, role playing, and taking turns. He joined in hand gestures to nursery rhymes and music around our piano, which usually escalated into dancing and jumping. In our backyard, he could play for hours alone with our dogs, a few sticks, and lots of mud!

As a father, it was very difficult to accept that my firstborn son could be considered "retarded" by others. It's a terrible stigma to live with. I understand that many fathers of special-needs children become embarrassed or ashamed of their child. I've even been told that the challenges of children with special needs cause a large percentage of those marriages to break up.

Instead of breaking us apart, Zachary's condition galvanized our marriage. It brought Melissa and me closer to each other and closer to God. It wasn't easy in any way. We had to work hard to keep a good family balance and to make time for each other, to go on dates, and to arrange babysitters who could care for a special-needs child. But it was a rich road that deepened tremendously the intimacy of our faith and our marriage. I wouldn't have traded my son or his challenges for anything.

It was inconceivable to me and Melissa that some people would consider aborting a child who *might* have Down syndrome, based on the often erroneous amniocentesis results. Those people unknowingly pass up a basketful of blessings in disguise. I considered my son's disability as a badge of honor that I wore with pride, as if to say, "See what daunting obstacles he's overcome? Yes, he's my son. I'm proud to be his father." I saw him as God's "workmanship" (Ephesians 2:10).

No amount of words or litany of therapies and hospital visits could contain the volumes of effort, letters, meetings, phone calls, heartaches, sleepless nights, prayers, and tears that Melissa poured into Zachary as his foremost advocate on this planet. She was stalwart in her efforts for him. Melissa loved Zachary with a bond and fervor only a mother could.

In fact, being a mother seemed to bring out the best in Melissa. It showed in how she treated our children each day, and also in her journal entries.

November 25, 1998
Happy Thanksgiving, my precious children. I give thanks this day, and every day for my precious family. You are each a special gift God has granted me to spend time, a lifetime, loving. I am so blessed to have you in my life. I

love you, my children. . . . I love you, Makenah, my big
girl. You mean the world to me. And my Zachary—you
have taught me to love like none other, my little ray of
sonshine where there looks like rain. My Makenah . . .
you are growing up before my very eyes, and there's
nothing I can do about it. I want you to grow, but I
don't because I want to spend years with you at this
age—this stage—every stage. I am baffled right now at
my overwhelming emotion about you. My Makenah, I
want to hold you, I want to cuddle you, I want to sing
to you, I want to cherish you. But you keep on growing,
the world keeps on going—and you aren't letting it pass
you by. Makenah, you changed my life when God
dropped you off in my heart. You keep changing me
more every day. And you're only three! . . . My son, my
Zachary, my lovebug. You brighten my life. You fill my
heart with joy. Your peace is overwhelming. Zachary, I
could watch you sleep. I want to cuddle you. I need your
love—your tender spirit ministers to me. Makenah, your
spirit teaches me new ways, so much. You minister to me,
my sweet girl. Zachary, my heart is filled with love for
you now, and always will be. My children, I cannot
believe I am your mother. I am so blessed to have you in
my life. I love you in a new way every day.

     —XO your Mommy

19

The Riptide

"Is Daddy at work?"

"Yes, he is, honey."

"Oh!"

My three-year-old asks this two, three, sometimes four times a day. I was just pondering if she will ever think Mommy's at work? She's only three, and of course I don't say to her when I get up: "Mommy's going to work now." Of course, Mommy doesn't bring home a paycheck to deposit into the bank. Daddy does that. Daddy works hard at least 40 hours a week for that paycheck and for that we are thankful. But I'm the Mommy. I'm the one who gets to work all day, all night (on call, of course). I don't get sick days. I get vacations, but they are like bringing work home with you.

That's okay because I'm the Mommy. I'm the Mommy whose payment comes in smiles and hugs and precious little people uttering "I wuv you, Mommy." Payment also comes in the form of being able to see my children take their first step—guaranteed!—and giving baths to the

cutest little naked bodies on earth. These are bigger
than any paycheck deposited into a bank, to me. These
are precious memories deposited in my heart. And little
do they know, they are so much work, if you wish to
label them a job. But they are the best job in the world.
     So, "Yes, baby, Daddy is at work, but Mommy loves
her job most!"
          —A note written by Melissa that Robert found after the flood

Right about the time Zachary was hospitalized for two weeks for aspiration pneumonia in February 1999, Makenah began adding some conspicuous words to our bedtime prayers. She kept praying for "Mommy's baby."

This was odd, because we weren't expecting again. We hoped to catch our breath after Zachary's harrowing first year. Eventually, however, Melissa started suspecting that Makenah's words might be right yet again. Sure enough, a home pregnancy test told her she was pregnant. We had another baby on the way! She was thrilled and shocked, since neither of us was expecting another pregnancy so soon after Zachary.

When I arrived home from work, Makenah was right at the kitchen door to greet me. She led me to the stairs where, unknown to me, Melissa was waiting at the top.

Then, Makenah made her announcement.

"Daddy! We're gonna have a baby!"

"What? Really?!" I shouted as I scooped up Makenah.

As I spun her around, I caught Melissa in my eye, smiling—no, beaming like a searchlight—at the top of the stairs. She had a big red bow wrapped around her like a belt. We hugged and danced together.

Eight months later, when it appeared we had another whopping nine-pounder in Melissa's belly, we went to North Kansas City Hospital to be induced. Melissa was determined to have another normal delivery. Yet hour after hour passed, all filled with consistent and intense contractions.

Once again, our faith and fortitude were tested. Despite all the lessons I thought I had learned through the years, I found myself questioning God and filled with fear. After almost 48 hours of hard labor contractions, Melissa's doctor finally said, "Melissa, let's do something else to get this baby out!"

At that point, we both finally relented.

At 5:13 P.M. on Saturday, October 9, 1999, Melissa got to announce this time, "It's . . . Nicholas!" We had another boy! Sure enough, he weighed in at a whopping nine pounds, one ounce, and 21 and a half inches long. He was absolutely beautiful and perfectly formed. He looked a lot like Makenah. I was thrilled to have a second son.

After two days of recovery, we brought Nicholas Adam home. Again, we were grateful to God for another beautiful child, and we were humbled at the reminder that God's plans may not be the same as ours, but His will is perfect.

I was concerned that having three children would divide my love for them into smaller portions. Instead, I learned that my love multiplied for them all. Plus, each of them received love from us *and* their siblings. As we had more children, there was simply more love to go around. Nicholas was a ray of sunshine that brightened our lives after all the trauma with Zachary. Melissa often sang "You Are My Sunshine" to him.

Nicholas was the essence of childhood: a cowboy always rounding up the bad guys. He lived for adventure with sticks and mud in our backyard and could make a gun out of a peanut butter sandwich.

He'd come barging through the doors with six-shooters a-blazing—and nail me right in the heart every time I heard him shout, "Hey, Dad!"

Early in January 2001, my engineering job required me to take a short business trip to Cancun for a sales meeting and training with a company that makes avionics cooling fans. It was a family-oriented company that encouraged us to bring our spouses and enjoy the afternoons together in the sun once the morning business meetings ended. I took Melissa while my sister Ellen watched our children.

Melissa and I were splashing around in the ocean when we noticed the surf was rougher than normal. We hadn't seen the red flags sporadically placed along the beach, which signify rough surf conditions—including possible riptides.

I grew up learning to swim at the local YMCA and at Rehoboth Beach, Delaware, every summer. I was very comfortable in the water. Swimming wasn't Melissa's strongest suit, but she knew how to tread water and stay afloat.

We had run into the ocean, laughing and splashing each other. We braved the water and gradually positioned ourselves out where the waves were breaking so that we could ride the next big one in. Without warning, our little spree in the surf turned into a wrestling match with the waves as we struggled to reach each cresting point. Our feet were dangling well above the ocean floor, and we were fighting just to stay afloat. We quickly ran out of energy and were coughing, gulping water, and gasping for air.

Our laughter turned to panic. I firmly held Melissa's wrist to keep her close. I tried to remain calm as I spun my legs in an egg-beater motion to stay afloat—something I had learned as a teenager at the YMCA. We glanced back at the shore and noticed that, without even realizing it, we were suddenly far away and being washed out to sea. Then it hit me. We were caught in a riptide! I knew that people drowned from riptides every year. They are like rivers in the ocean that suck you out to sea. My brother Jeff was caught in one in the Atlantic Ocean and nearly drowned.

I wasn't thinking clearly enough to remember that because riptides are circular, the best way out of them is to swim parallel to the shore. Instead, I instinctively flipped to my side, held Melissa's wrist, and swam sidestroke with all my might toward the shore to get us in. But I didn't seem to be making any progress. Unknown to us, there was a commotion gathering on the shore as people realized we were drifting away and struggling just to stay alive.

We thought we were on the verge of drowning. We could barely keep our mouths above the water long enough to catch a quick breath. I heard Melissa call out faintly, "Robert, let me go . . ."

"What?" I shouted through the salty mist.

"Let me go! Just let me go." Melissa struggled between breaths and gulps just to squeak out those words.

"No way! I can't!"

"Our kids need one good parent, and you can make it back without me. But we're both going to drown out here."

I couldn't believe my ears. She was willing to sacrifice her own life for the sake of our children.

"Just let me go," she cried out.

"No way, Melissa!"

I couldn't do it. I couldn't let go of the love of my life. I swam harder and harder against the pounding surf. We were making incremental progress, but the tide was so turbulent that the shoreline seemed to keep shifting. I held even tighter onto Melissa's wrist and kept swimming sidestroke.

Just then a lifeguard reached us from out of nowhere. He had a rope wrapped around him attached to a red life preserver. "Grab on!" he shouted. I pulled Melissa forward and placed her hands on the side of the life preserver and then held on myself. I kept whipping my legs with the little energy I had left. He had rescued us just in time.

He pulled us the rest of the way in, and we collapsed on the sandy shore in sheer exhaustion. We were in shock at what had just transpired. In just a matter of minutes, an innocent afternoon of frolicking in the waves nearly turned fatal. We tearfully embraced each other on the sand. We longed to be home and hug our kids. Melissa and I were thankful just to be alive. I had learned the full depth of her love for our children: She was willing to lay down her own life for them.

We went to our room, got on our knees, and cried in thanksgiving to God that we were okay. It strengthened our faith even further. There was no question that His hand was upon us in the water, keeping us from death. It also strengthened our resolve to keep praying for our children. It proved to us that they were specially chosen by God. If the Enemy was trying this hard to disrupt their lives—from conception, through the hours of labor and delivery, and even now in the riptide—then our children were indeed "mighty in the land" as Psalm 112:2 says. We were convinced that each of them had great things to do on this earth and would touch many lives.

20

The Journey of Love

Shortly after our 10th wedding anniversary, Melissa gleefully announced to me, "We're going to have another baby!"

We were thrilled. Number four was on the way! He or she would be born in the fall. We were overflowing with joy at the news. But a few weeks later, I found Melissa sobbing in the bathroom with her head buried in her hands. I crouched down and held her in my arms.

"What's wrong, bubby?"

She could barely speak through her tears: "I lost our baby!"

We cried together. It was the second time during our marriage that we had suffered a miscarriage. We ached for our lost child. This latest loss was effectively our fifth encounter with death: two miscarriages, Melissa's ectopic rupture, our close call in the riptide, and the surrender of the son we were expecting when God gave us Zachary. Looking back, it became clear to me that God was forging our faith all along and grooming us for something incredible—something that would require a tremendous amount of patience, fortitude, trust, and perseverance in the midst of adversity.

Even before Melissa announced that we were pregnant with Baby Joy, we had discussed adoption. After this second miscarriage, we searched our hearts and encountered something embedded deeply in each of us: a desire to adopt. I believed it was the Holy Spirit speaking to each of us individually. We were both already hoping to have another daughter, and Makenah made it clear to us how much she wanted a sister when she said, "We already have too much boys!"

We reflected on China's "one child per family" policy, which in practice resulted in girls accounting for 95 percent of the adopted orphans.[1] That tore at our hearts. In February 2002, we went to an informational meeting at Children's Hope International in Kansas City. Before the meeting was over, we knew we wanted to do this. Our daughter was somewhere out there, already waiting for us. She would not be just any child, either: We sensed we were called to adopt a special-needs child.

We believed that God had prepared us to deal with special-needs children through Zachary. We had learned that imperfections were God's way of demonstrating His perfection and strength in our lives and that incredible blessings could come through periods of absolute brokenness. We saw the genuine smile affixed to Zachary's face. It was undeniable to us now that the fruit of such intense toil and heartache was even sweeter when you had to work so hard to harvest it.

People warned us that international adoption was difficult, and they were right! The process sifts out anyone who lacks the fortitude and perseverance to complete an adoption and raise such a special child. For 11 months, Melissa attacked the mound of paperwork like a bulldog. Meanwhile, I was taking night classes to earn my Master of Business Administration degree. It was a journey that stretched out for more than five years. I burned the midnight oil many nights so that I only sacrificed my own sleep and not time with my family.

Melissa and I had short fuses during many of those months of adoption paperwork, and we had to extend large measures of grace and forgiveness to each other. Always, it seemed, there was the waiting: for approval from the Chinese Center of Adoption Affairs, for our official date to travel to China, and for just the right child.

The agency called on September 12, 2002, with news of a waiting child. When Melissa gazed at the pictures of Guo Wen Ying—an orphan girl with pulmonary stenosis, a heart defect—she was so moved she wept with the other women at the agency. Melissa grabbed the pictures and paperwork and sped to my office. She startled me as she unexpectedly barged through the company door with Nicholas in tow. Right away, I could tell from the traces of tears around her eyes that this was big.

"Robert, meet our new daughter . . ." She proudly held up the pictures, and I fell back into my chair as I gazed in awe at God's newest gift to us. I gripped the pictures. She was beautiful. We both knew this little girl was destined to be our daughter. We shared tears of joy, knowing that our journey of love to China was near. We learned that her Chinese name, *Wen Ying*, meant "intelligent and beautiful." We wanted to keep her name as part of her Chinese heritage, so we combined it with a name we had chosen: Alenah WenYing Rogers.

We were scheduled to depart for China on January 2. Our 11th wedding anniversary on New Year's Eve was simple and low-key. We were too excited and busy with the adoption to do anything fancy. We were up until 2:00 A.M. on the morning of our departure packing our bags, checking and rechecking our list of travel documents, and gathering baby clothes, gifts, and other necessities. As we walked down the Jetway to board the Boeing 747, we exchanged glances, took a deep breath, and said, "This is it!"

It was just the two of us. We still had to meet all the right escorts at three Chinese airports and make all the connecting flights. One little mishap, slipup, illness, lost passport, lost piece of luggage, or overlooked piece of paperwork could jeopardize the entire mission. We landed in Beijing, met our escort, and checked into the hotel for the night. We were anxious the entire two weeks, hoping that everything would go smoothly.

On top of all that, we were carrying around thousands of dollars in cash for the adoption. It took a tremendous measure of faith for us to make this trip. Our journey was not without risks, but the risks were all worth it.

On January 5, we flew from Beijing to Changsha in the Hunan Province. It was a city of several million people and extremely crowded. We checked into the hotel and took the elevator up to our room. This was the day we would receive our daughter! In fact, within minutes of checking in, our room phone rang. It was our guide telling us that she was on her way up to our room with our baby!

I slammed the phone down. "She's on her way!" We hadn't even unpacked yet. We frantically and tearfully bustled around the room. The doorbell rang, and Melissa screamed. I started the camcorder in the corner of the room and dashed for the door. I let Melissa be the first to receive our new daughter. As I slowly opened the door, we heard the words, "The baby is coming!" Our tears gushed and my heart melted the minute I set eyes on our bundle of love.

Alenah WenYing was more beautiful than I had ever imagined. We held her and rocked her as our guide filled out paperwork and spoke with the director and auntie from the Zhuzhou Children's Welfare Institute—her orphanage about 100 miles away. I couldn't take my eyes off our daughter. I sang to her, placed my hand on her forehead, and blessed her as we waited for our guests to leave the room so we could just be alone with her. Alenah was timid and shy at first. She was just over a year old, and she cried as she was separated from the only caregivers she had ever known. As they left the room, Melissa and I embraced Alenah in sheer delight. After all this time, she was finally ours.

Next to seeing Melissa give birth, it was the most amazing feeling I had ever experienced. Alenah took her first bottle well and slept all the way through the first night. The next morning, she woke up a new child—standing in her crib, holding on to the sides, and bouncing ever so slightly—all smiles and happy to see us. All our fears and apprehension washed away at that moment. All the preparation, the forms, and every dollar were worth it.

We finalized the adoption process over the next eight days and visited Alenah's orphanage. Melissa would write about the experience to Alenah in her journal:

Tuesday, January 7, 2003, 4:00 P.M.
Nothing can even explain the burden I feel here. . . . I cannot believe you have done so well in these conditions. We thank the director. I am overwhelmed with emotion and cry. I am sure this is not proper—but I cannot contain my emotion—the sheer gratitude for the care they gave you and our ability to take you away from this. And then there are the children left behind—some will never be adopted. Those children have an unpredictable future. This is the reason I cannot contain it all . . . If we had not followed our hearts, would you be one of those children? I thank God He spoke to us and gave us our desire—a precious gift we

are grateful for no matter <u>how</u> you were born into our family—you were born in our hearts and that is the first place your brothers and sister were too. We love you all so deeply. Thank You, Lord, for the most precious gifts we will ever receive: our Makenah, Zachary, Nicholas, and Alenah!

We bought 17 meaningful Chinese gifts as birthday presents for Alenah for the next 17 years—as a way of acknowledging and honoring her Chinese heritage. Finally, on January 15, we boarded a huge Boeing 777 with many other adoptive families, all eager to touch American soil and be home again. As the plane approached Los Angeles International Airport, the adoptive families erupted into applause. There's nothing quite like coming home.

The next day, we flew through Minneapolis and home to Kansas City. We were the last ones to come through the gate doors and into the terminal. From a distance, I spotted Makenah jumping up and down next to her brothers. Oh, what a glorious sight they were! We were greeted by a burst of tears and cheers from Jere, Judy, my parents, our neighbors, and many others. We ran to them and clustered into a giant hug.

Then came the moment that would stay in my memory and come back to me later: Melissa hugged my sister Anne tightly in appreciation for taking care of our three children and whispered in her ear, "I'll never leave them like that again—ever."

We braved the elements outside to the car. Ten inches of snow had fallen the night before, and all the schools were closed. What a beautiful white blanket over the Missouri countryside to commemorate our homecoming! We arrived home 30 minutes later and entered through the front door with Alenah for the first time. We crossed the threshold and embraced each other once again. The journey of love was now complete: We were home.

That Sunday, we took Alenah to church, and everyone hovered over her. We dedicated her to God and prayed with Pastor Jerls and the elders that God would heal her congenital heart defect. Several weeks later, Melissa took Alenah to Children's Mercy Hospital to check her heart. To our shocked delight, the cardiologist said, "Well, bring her back in a year. I don't think she'll ever need surgery." She wouldn't need a corrective balloon procedure or open-heart surgery after all! God was so good.

21

A Glorious Summer

It's a windy, overcast spring day, and the three little ones are still in jammies. I thought about going to the zoo today, but tomorrow will be better. . . . Nicholas is "coldy," and he's running around with a blanket wrapped around him. I think Zachary is chomping at the bit to go outside. Alenah is content to play with toys . . . she's so peaceful . . . sometimes needy—but who isn't? All Nicholas can talk about is good and bad guys. He wants to get the bad guys, so I told him he can be a policeman when he grows up. He was pretty excited to do that so he can get the bad guys! Right now, Alenah is playing with balls, throwing them and chasing them. It's amazing how well she is doing. It's hard to believe it was three months ago we landed in Beijing on an adventure of a lifetime. . . . She mesmerizes people wherever we go. She is so precious. Thank You, God. She is a gift we are so thankful for. Just like Makenah, Zachary, and Nicholas. I was thinking last night how God really knows what we need, when we need it. Makenah is so

*sweet, compassionate, and helpful. Her birth was a very
difficult one, though. And then Zachary came along,
and God gave me a natural delivery so I could be with
my son when he needed me most. And along came
Nicholas. Well, he was a tough one to get here, but with
two little boys, I'm so glad God gave us Makenah first!
And Nicholas is so funny and capable. I've always said
he was the kind of baby that was easy to forget you had
him. He was so quiet and watchful. . . . Now they're so
close and have so much fun together. And they're fulfill-
ing their roles as big brothers to Alenah—bossy, loving,
protective, and they pick on her too. Life is good with
four kids—not too different than three. But number five
or six is moved out, so we can have some sanity time . . .
we'll see what God does next!*

—Melissa's final journal entry, April 2003

During what turned out to be our last summer, we pulled back
from a lot of our normal extracurricular activities. I refrained from
night-school classes for three months. We pulled our children out
of music and dance classes, and we didn't plan any big family vacation. We just wanted to relax as a family with the freedom to be
spontaneous.

On a moment's notice, we went camping, hiking, biking, fish-
ing, or walking. We baked dozens of chocolate-chip cookies, zipped
to Sonic for ice cream treats, went roller skating, checked out books
and videos from the library, took in Royals baseball games, played
rounds of miniature golf, and capped off muggy days with a swim in
our little inflatable pool on the back deck. We savored ice cream and

Popsicles on the front porch. Melissa and I swayed in the swing while the kids played in the front yard. We even enjoyed a few calm rainstorms as our children ran from the safe, dry confines of the porch out into the teeming rain pouring down and overflowing from the gutters above.

In short, we made memories—as Melissa so often urged us to do. We were picture fanatics and took scores of them over the years, especially our final summer together. One of our favorite things to do after we put our kids to bed was to snuggle up together on the sofa with a dish of ice cream and a new pack of pictures. Melissa was patient enough after she bought them not to open the envelope until we could go through them together at night. It was a time we relished together.

At times that summer, I would just sit back and smile as I gazed upon the family God had given me: a gorgeous wife of nearly 12 years and four beautiful children. They were a ton of work, but they were all so worth it. God had blessed me beyond anything I could have dreamed. With Zachary's behavior now under control, and with far fewer life stresses as our older kids became more independent, Melissa remarked more than once, "I've had the best summer ever with our kids." It was a magical time together.

We had driven to Cincinnati at Easter to introduce Alenah to the rest of my family. Then, on August 1, we drove back to Cincinnati again for the weekend. We knew school would start soon, and we wanted to have one last fun road trip for the summer and visit family.

We had a wonderful time grilling hamburgers and playing in the lake with cousins and aunts and uncles. When it was time to head home, we migrated from our van to their cars three times just to get more hugs. There was just something about that visit that was extra special. My father finally got to walk proudly through his neighborhood with Zachary—hand in hand—a dream he had held in his heart since Zachary's Down syndrome diagnosis.

Had we not followed our hearts and impulsively driven the 600 miles to Cincinnati, we would have missed a very special set of last memories together. I felt that the Holy Spirit prompted us to go. It wasn't something we normally would have done over a short weekend.

Two weeks later, my oldest brother, Paul, and his family were passing through Kansas City on their way from Branson, Missouri, to Rochester, Minnesota. We all went out for pizza and visited for a long time. Again, we seemed to say three full rounds of good-byes—once in the restaurant, once outside the door, and once by the cars—as we took even more pictures. Looking back, there was just something tugging at our spirits, urging us to savor these final moments with one another.

Two weeks later, my siblings were back in Kansas City—for my family's funeral.

22

Surrounded by Memories

Wednesday, September 3, 2003

As I came out of my long reverie, commotion downstairs told me that hours had passed and people were now gathering. I got up, dressed, and slowly descended the stairs. By now, all seven of my siblings and their families were in town and staying in nearby hotels. We formed a circle and put our arms around each other's shoulders. Feeling the enormity of all that had happened already, and realizing what still remained ahead of us, we closed our eyes and prayed.

I found myself wanting to linger quietly around our home before the busyness of the day set in. I sat down at the kitchen table where we last ate pancakes together on Saturday morning. My body trembled as I recognized that the baby's high chair and the other four chairs were now empty. My hands touched the places where the table had endured plenty of spills and nicks over the years. Our kitchen table was a gravitational force for our family—a place where we drew closer to each other. It was a place that fostered memories and conversation and eye contact for our family. We'd spent so much time there—celebrating birthdays, enjoying pizza parties, sharing meals and conversation regularly.

I peered through the kitchen windows into the backyard. I saw the deck, the patio, and the swing set. I got up from the kitchen table and made my way through the laundry room out to the deck. There were clothes still hanging on the collapsible wooden drying racks in the laundry room—little socks, T-shirts, and other summertime clothes.

I slowly and somberly walked through the door and out onto the sun-bleached wooden deck and concrete patio. Our backyard, surrounded by a six-foot cedar privacy fence we built shortly after we moved in, was our children's world. It was a refuge of playtime, swing time, sled rides, sprinklers, bumps, bruises, baseball, mud, and fireflies.

Our two dogs, Ira and Amadeus—a white rat terrier with black spots and a blond cocker spaniel—seemed excited to see me but confused not to see our children, their longtime playmates. The dogs had grown attached and accustomed to all the attention from our children, especially Zachary. He would play for hours in the backyard, giggling with the dogs, pulling at their fur, and letting Ira lick his face from top to bottom.

I descended the grassy hill to the swing set and felt my stomach tighten once again. The swing set was older and slightly rusted. One of the seats was dangling by a chain. The other side had broken from all the use, and I just hadn't fixed it yet. Still, it didn't stop our kids. Makenah would prop her feet on the seat where the good chain was still attached, stand upright, grab the chain with both hands, and gleefully swing away.

The stained cedar fence had bare spots on it from where Zachary would bump it over and over when he rode the glider swing and got going so fast, giggling so loud we could hear him from the kitchen every time he bumped the fence. He was fearless, scaling the swing valiantly with absolutely no concept of danger.

I knelt down by the swing set now, weeping as I reverently ran my fingers over these blue pieces of plastic that my children had touched so many times. My T-shirt was soaked with my tears; I could not stop crying. I wanted to keep touching the swings until I could embrace my children. But I knew it would never happen. I saw the red baby swing suspended from the grand silver maple tree behind the deck. I could barely stand to watch it swing back and forth on its own—empty—as I pictured each of our children, one by one, swinging there in the early years of their lives. They all grew into and out of that old, red baby swing.

I still hadn't shaved or showered in four days, so I finally stood and went back inside, climbed the stairs, and made my way into the tiny bathroom we all shared. Our children's toothbrushes were suspended from the mirror-mounted holders. How could I face this bathroom and this mirror alone day after day?

Nevertheless, it felt good to shave and have that clean feeling over my face. Staring at myself in the mirror, I already sensed that I looked like a different person. I stepped into the shower and hesitated to stand under the showerhead. I hadn't experienced water rushing over me in any way since the flood. It startled me for a moment, but then it felt refreshing, reviving, and renewing.

Then I turned around.

Our children's washcloths hung on the towel rack at the far end of the shower where we always kept them. I touched them, and chills rippled through my body. I turned my head away to face the showerhead and was caught by the sight of Melissa's washcloth next to mine. Tears washed down my face. I cried uncontrollably, my cries turning into groans of deep agony. I later learned that all through-out the house my family could hear my sobs. My heart was broken. I placed my hand on the wall to keep from falling as I wept.

The day was just starting, and already I felt drained. *Dear God, fill me up,* I prayed. *There's no possible way I can do this on my own.*

Over time, I discovered that as I emptied myself of me, through endless tears and constant surrender, God filled me up with Him. His sustaining power was undeniable. It was the *only* thing getting me through this ordeal.

The rest of the day became chaotic: visitors coming in and out of our home all day; people asking to speak with me on the phone, in the driveway, and out by the memorial; people just needing to hug me to help them mourn and see for themselves that what they saw on the news had really happened. I was blessed to receive over-whelming generosity: people bringing food, offering to clean the house and mow the lawn. Flowers and teddy bears were arriving nearly every hour. Food baskets arrived from CBS and *The John Walsh Show*. People were coordinating trips to the airport to pick up relatives and friends arriving in town.

There were myriad details to attend to: end-of-the-month bills and volumes of condolence letters arriving in the mail, insurance paperwork and visits from our State Farm agent, the press confer-ence at the church that evening, and the candlelight vigil in our front yard that night. Most painful of all were looming visits to the funeral home to plan the arrangements and to the cemetery to pick out the five grave sites.

On top of all that, there was intense media interest, both locally and nationally. My brother George had been fielding countless interview requests from the major news networks. He felt most comfortable with the gracious attitude and demeanor of the folks at

CBS's *The Early Show*. We agreed to a live remote interview with Hannah Storm for Friday morning right after the 6:00 newscast. The satellite truck would be at my home at 4:00 to set up. Our family visitation would be Friday night, and the public visitation, funeral, and burial would be Saturday morning.

I was quickly overwhelmed by all these compounding details. On top of my own grief, I was also witnessing it around me all day long and receiving it through the heartfelt embraces of so many visitors. It felt as if they were transferring their grief into me, as though I were drinking sorrow through a fire hose.

I was experiencing firsthand the truth that in our weakness, God is strong. When we become nothing, He can become everything. From moment to moment, I was clinging to God with every fiber of my being.

I never felt as if I needed to be strong for everyone. And yet I somehow remained in control of my actions and of all the logistical details throughout the week. I didn't collapse or crumble. I can only describe it as a miracle of God's grace and strength working through me in my time of absolute weakness. As a confirmed introvert, I still did the bulk of my grieving alone.

Perhaps there was some measure of adrenaline involved in my enduring strength and determination, yet nothing but God's strong right hand could have sustained me and held me through such an intense ordeal.

I heard so many times from so many people, "God never gives you more than you can handle." I eventually came to believe that "God will always give you more than you can bear alone, because He doesn't want you to bear it without Him." Alone, this cross was unbearable. But with God, it was possible.

23

No Regrets

A police car came by our home to take us to the church for the 4:00 P.M. press conference. Few words were spoken as my parents and I made the two-mile journey to the church.

Every other time I had pulled into the church parking lot over the past six years, Melissa or one of our kids had been with me. Now, it was only me.

We were ushered through the back door straight to the chapel, where everyone was already assembled and waiting. Just 10 days earlier, at our last church service together as a family, Pastor Jerls had invited people forward for prayer. Our entire family, all six of us, went forward. Melissa, Makenah, and I knelt by the altar, clutching Zachary, Nicholas, and Alenah in our arms and praying for God's blessings, healing, and protection over us. People laid hands on us and prayed for our family.

The irony of that last family gathering in this church lingered heavily as we met pastors and staff in the hallway. We huddled for a quick prayer before the press conference began. I lifted my head, straightened my back, took a deep breath, and focused on the

moment at hand. Someone opened the door, and the sight of cameras, flashes, and reporters unfolded in front of me. I was filled with
some anticipation but not anxiety about being in front of cameras. I
was totally at peace.

Our mayor was already at the podium, in front of all the microphones, introducing me. I looked into the cameras intently and
started reading my words. As soon as I reached the part about
Melissa's fate and said, "She did not survive the tragedy," my voice
broke, and I could barely contain my emotion.

"She was the love of my life and meant more than this world to
me," I said, somehow finding the strength to continue. I spoke of
how we met, our courtship, and our marriage.

"We seized many moments in time and passionately enjoyed life
together," I said. "I have no regrets."

I talked about what happened the night my family was taken
from me.

"It's truly a miracle that I am alive and standing before you right
now, with only a few minor scrapes and bruises," I said. "I *know* that
there is a God and that He loves us—and He wants us to live with
Him . . . God gave His only Son so that we could. When God is our
refuge, even when there is despair, there is hope! Even in the midst
of sorrow, there is peace and joy!"

I talked of how difficult my first visit home was, with its silence
and emptiness.

"This tragedy may have shattered my family, but it will not shat-
ter my resolve to hope for good," I said. "We live in a fallen world. It
rains on the just and the unjust alike. Evil seeks only to steal, kill, and
destroy. But God came that we might have life—more abundantly.
To honor the memory of my wife and children with something

positive out of this terrible tragedy, please love, cherish, and savor your families every day. Hug and play with them. Eat meals and pray together, and tell your family you love them every day."

I shared different ways families could reach out to other ministries and then I closed with a final point: "I'm not bitter against God. I've had a full, abundant life, and I'm fully persuaded that somehow, by His grace, He will turn this tragedy into good. He has graced me with a blessed, abundant life. Now, He has given my wife and children a blessed and abundant life everlasting."

I finished my words and walked directly to the back of the room, out of the chapel, down the hallway, and out of the church toward the police car. Normally, given my shy nature, I would have been shaking from all the jitters of the moment. Yet I carried a peaceful resolve from God that was nothing short of miraculous. Some even remarked later that my countenance radiated the peace and glory of God.

We arrived home, and I was startled to be greeted by hugs and affection from my siblings and relatives. I learned that the press conference had been aired live, and they had gathered around the television in the family room to watch it. The local FOX affiliate received so many calls from people who missed the first airing that they decided to show both of my press conferences—the one Monday in Emporia and now Wednesday in Liberty—in their entirety at the beginning of the 5:00 P.M. newscast.

I was stunned and amazed at God. It was as if, just four days after that awful night, God was being glorified and people's lives were being changed for the better through my family. It came at such a high cost. And yet God was already proving to me that He could indeed work all things for good, no matter how bad they might be.

At the end of the broadcast, they announced the candlelight vigil at my home and even displayed a map of the neighborhood showing directions to my house. The tempo of activity at home accelerated as the evening approached. The crowd began gathering well before the vigil began. My home filled with people passing through, exchanging hugs, leaving food, taking food, getting a drink, and even using the restroom. It was unsettling to lose every sense of privacy and any hint of "normalcy" inside my home. With my face all over televisions and newspapers, and now with my home address plastered on the TV screen for all to see, I felt terribly vulnerable.

Amid the flurry of people passing through my home, I came face-to-face with Liz and Tom—Melissa's mother and stepfather. It had been months since we had last seen each other. They didn't go to Emporia during the search and recovery, and we were never able to connect by phone.

We hugged, and I could see the devastation in their eyes. We had moved our family from California to Kansas City six years earlier because we wanted to be close to Melissa's family. Yet because of the demanding responsibilities on their farm, we had not seen as much of Liz and Tom over the years as we would have liked.

Now, as we stood in the hallway of my house with everyone buzzing around us, Liz said to me words I'll never forget.

"I regret not coming to visit more often."

I regret . . .

It was the antithesis of what I had just finished saying in my press conference to the cameras a few hours ago: "I have no regrets." The contrast of our words was stark. I was overwhelmed by my family's deaths, but I was free from the pain of regret.

I reassured her, "They knew you loved them. In fact, the night of the flood they were sleeping with the quilts you made for them."

It was true. Our kids loved the quilts she had handmade for

them. They were soft and warm and went with us on every family road trip. Liz was still working on Alenah's quilt at the time of the flood.

As I reflected back on our lives, I realized that we truly lived a life of no regrets. It wasn't that we lived a perfect life. We messed up plenty of times, and I stuck both feet in my mouth more often than I care to count. But, as a whole, our family time was so special and our life was so good because we intentionally made rich memories and made a point of living life to the fullest.

Despite all the tragedy that had just befallen me, I still felt deeply thankful to God for all the years I had had with Melissa and our children. I felt blessed to have lived such a full life of faith and family. That moment with Liz simply reinforced a desire that was blossoming in my heart: to challenge and teach others to live that kind of life—a life of no regrets.

I sensed this was my calling now. This was the living tribute of Melissa and our children to the world—a timeless message about God and families. In retrospect, this day and these moments were the genesis of my ministry.

Nightfall descended, and our neighbor Mica lit all the candles around the side-yard memorial. People from church, Zachary's pre-school, Makenah's grade school and dance academy, Melissa's water aerobics class, our adoption agency, the surrounding communities, and many people I didn't even know poured into our front and side yards until it looked like a sea of faces. Estimates put the crowd at more than 500.

Photographers with huge lenses on their cameras mounted on tripods and live news vans lined the street. A policeman, his car lights flashing, was diverting and directing traffic. The vigil began at 8:30 P.M. Our American flag hung lifeless in the stillness of the humid summer air. We were all congregating where, just a week ago, my children had been eating Popsicles, catching fireflies, riding bikes, and shooting hoops with Melissa and me. The irony of these starkly contrasting images devastated me.

Several boxes of candles made their way around the crowd. As the candles were lit, my entire yard flickered with warm light, casting a soft glow on the faces of everyone. Our pastor's wife and minister of music led us in choruses of "Jesus Loves Me" and "Amazing Grace." Then my friend Tony Ceballos, the drummer from our church, stood on a small footstool and spoke into the microphone.

"It is fitting for us to use candles tonight because they illuminate life. You are the way, Jesus, the truth, and the life. Just as light dissipates darkness, so did the smiles of Melissa and the kids. They've all affected our lives, and even if you didn't know them personally, they've affected you, or else you wouldn't be here.

"Don't wait until the next candlelight vigil to pay respect to the people in your lives. We are shallow if we can't walk up to a spouse, our children—God's gifts to us—and say 'I love you.' What Robert wouldn't give to be in your place right now. . . . Celebrate the living while they're here. Make that phone call to that relative you haven't talked to in 10 years because they looked at you funny one Christmas."

Tony urged others to trust Jesus as their Lord and Savior, because none of us is guaranteed tomorrow. Then he turned the microphone over to me.

"I'm standing only because God is holding me up," I told the crowd. "This is about eternity. I will see them soon someday."

The prayer vigil lasted perhaps half an hour. As people dispersed, hugging one another and crying, the MercyMe song "I Can Only Imagine" was played over the sound system. I learned later that after the vigil, several reporters were asking my neighbors, "What's Robert *really* like? I mean, is he for real?" They just responded, "What you see is really the way he is. That's him, for real."

A line of people materialized where I was standing. I stayed and hugged and cried with every person until everyone had left. It was after 10:00 P.M. by then. Exhausted, I went upstairs, crawled into Makenah's bed, and wept.

24

*A Final
Resting Place*

The hectic pace and intense moment-to-moment grief resumed on Thursday. Visitors, flowers, and huge stacks of mail continued to pour in. We had made appointments at the funeral home and cemetery to finalize arrangements for the funeral. My sisters combed the house, gathering mementos for the memorial floral arrangements. They also gathered clothes to bury my family in. I felt overwhelmed at the thought of such a task. I just wanted them to look as they would on a typical day.

My parents, my best friends, and several of my siblings came with me to the funeral home. I was never comfortable inside funeral homes. They always gave me the creeps. I had never liked being close to dead bodies. Now, I had to face all my worst fears at once. We met with Nevin, the funeral home director, and discussed the details of the funeral. I had to fill out paperwork and choose caskets. Answering questions about Melissa and our children, choosing five white caskets—the entire process felt surreal and unnatural.

Next, we drove to Glenridge, a cemetery a few miles past downtown Liberty. When we arrived and I set foot on the ground, I just knew that this was the right place. Glenridge, nestled in the country past several train trestles, was a beautiful, serene setting: gentle rolling hills, pastureland, graceful oak trees, and a small cemetery surrounded by a single circular drive.

The feature that struck me most was the calm, peaceful pond just a few yards away. I was reminded of the flood site, because of the water and rolling hills. Yet it was also reminiscent of Melissa's family farm in northeast Kansas. There were cows in the distance grazing in the fields. We heard an occasional "moo" through the quiet serenity. It reminded me so much of my first trip to Hiawatha to meet Melissa's folks in 1990, shortly before I proposed to her. She taught me then how to appreciate the simple beauty of pastures and even cows mooing in the distance.

The setting for this cemetery embodied a microcosm of our lives—from beginning to end—and of Scripture from Psalm 23: "The LORD is my Shepherd; I shall not want. He makes me lie down in green pastures. He leads me beside still waters. He restores my soul" (verses 1–3, ESV).

These green pastures would be the final resting place for my family. God led me out of and beside the waters that night of the flash flood. Now He led me to this small body of still waters. And as we quietly stood there, I sensed that He was restoring my soul. I felt warmth deep within, as if there was something about home to this place. It was right.

We chose six plots in a row, near the base of a young, strong pin oak. It felt good to have these decisions settled. It felt as if God was providing for our every need.

Thursday continued to be overwhelming with many details to tend to for my family's funeral on Saturday, plus people arriving from out of town and others streaming through my home constantly. I tried to get to bed earlier on Thursday night since the CBS *Early Show* crew would be arriving at 4:00 A.M. to set up the satellite remote.

I suppose I shouldn't have been surprised when my mom, dad, and several brothers were already up and going with me by four o'clock the next morning. We greeted the film crew in the darkness and led them to the living room with the Steinway piano. While the crew was setting up, I stayed in Makenah's room and prayed on her bed, asking God to give me the words to speak. I wasn't nervous or afraid. I still had total peace. I had already faced my worst fear in life. This was nothing compared to that.

I showered, dressed in an open-collar, blue dress shirt, and came downstairs. The living room had grown warm from all the activity and heat from all the lights. My oldest brother, Paul, was pacing the house, placing his hand on my shoulder and praying for me from time to time. My parents were seated in chairs in the front entryway where they were out of the crew's way but still had a good view of everything.

The crew members wired me with the microphone, and I sat on the edge of my piano bench, since I was most comfortable there—behind the keyboard. I could hear the New York CBS headquarters in my earpiece, but I couldn't see anything. We had no video monitor. Hannah Storm was about to interview me. Shortly after 6:00 A.M. central time, I heard the top news stories and the national weather through my earpiece.

I could feel my heart pounding harder as they approached the end of the weather. They played an introductory piece, and then Hannah began asking me questions. I wasn't afraid. I was direct, transparent, and succinct. I emphasized that I felt I was still alive as a banner of hope and a beacon for families. The few minutes seemed to go by very quickly.

At the end of the interview, Hannah spoke with me for nearly 30 seconds through the earpiece. She expressed her sincere condolences and their overwhelming sentiment that they were all inspired and amazed by my attitude and apparent strength through this ordeal. I thanked Hannah for the gracious way that she and all the CBS crew had treated my family and me.

Then one of the crew technicians said something I'll never forget.

"Mr. Rogers, I'm not a religious man. But now, after witnessing this, I want to be."

It was apparent that already this testimony of God's grace through my life was penetrating hearts around the country—starting in my own living room and radiating out like ripples in a pond.

We were all relieved that the interview went smoothly, and we breathed a sigh of relief when the satellite truck pulled out of the driveway. We still had a full day of details and preparation for the funeral. Worst of all, we still faced the private family visitation that night at the funeral home. I would finally get to see all my family together—one last time.

25

Five White Coffins

I had been dreading this moment all day, and yet it was staring me in the face before I knew it.

We made the 10-minute drive to the funeral home. There was a smattering of conversation in the lobby as family members struggled to face the reality that this tragedy had claimed the lives of five people close to them.

The last time many of them had seen us was at a family reunion celebrating my parents' 50th wedding anniversary in 2002, which Melissa and I had hosted at our home. As we were taking family pictures together, I had said, "Savor this time together, everyone. It could be the last time we're all together." I was thinking that nieces and nephews would be going off to college and getting married, and the likelihood of us all meeting again at one time in one place was remote at best. Little did I know that one year later we'd all be gathered again—but this time for a funeral.

My family's.

Nevin came to me and said, "Robert, it's time."

I stood motionless for a moment and felt my feet stick to the floor. My blood drained to my toes. I took a deep breath and found my voice.

"Okay. I'm ready. I'd like to be alone with them first."

I took another deep breath and followed Nevin through a set of double doors. My body was cold and shaking. And then, for the first time in six days, I finally saw them all together.

Five white caskets were lined up end to end, wrapped around the end of the long, narrow room. They were arranged almost in a half circle because there wasn't enough room to place them in a straight line. All five of the caskets were open.

First on the left was Nicholas, then Zachary. Melissa was in the center, followed by Makenah, then Alenah on the far right. I inched my way down the aisle, my feet growing heavier by the second. It was as if they were trying to keep me from the unbearable.

"I'll be here if you need me," Nevin said gently, then he went out the back doors and closed them behind him.

I was alone.

I dropped to my knees in the center of the half circle and stretched out my arms open wide. I tilted my head back, looked up toward heaven, and cried out, "Oh, God. Oh, God! Whyyyyyyyyy?!! Why, God?!!"

I curled up in a fetal position on the floor as tears streamed down my cheeks.

Just one week before, at this very hour, all six of us were enjoying a night of popcorn, pizza, movies, and ice cream. Now this. How could something so sudden and random wipe out the people who were most precious to me on this planet, and leave me alive to bear the pain alone? Why was I still alive? So many unanswered questions still ran through my mind.

I slowly stood and approached Melissa first. She looked nothing like herself. What remained was only an outer shell—as if she had taken off a jacket and left it behind. I had to pull myself away. It was more than I could bear.

"I love you, bubby. I shall always love you, Melissa. Good night, sweetheart. Sweet dreams."

I couldn't find any other words to say to her. I felt as though I had said them all throughout our lifetime. I moved to my son Zachary. He looked perfect—almost as if he had never had Down syndrome. His eyes were gently closed, and his glasses were back on his face. His hands were folded on his chest over his red soccer-ball shirt—complete with worn marks and indelible grass stains. His fine blond hair was brushed off to one side.

"I love you, my son," I told him. "You're healed now. No more chains to hold you back. You can speak and sing with the angels with reckless abandon."

I reverently stepped to the far left and hovered over Nicholas. He looked perfect too—as if he were about to leap out of the casket and yell, "Hey, Dad, can we play baseball in the backyard?" Oh, how I ached to hear those words just one more time from him. I looked beyond his gently folded hands, and there around his waist was a holster with two plastic six-shooters on either side. I couldn't help but crack a little smile. It was so like Nicholas. I needed that dash of humor to puncture this heaviness.

"Thanks, buddy boy," I said to him. "I love you. I shall always love you, Nicholas. Go with Jesus, pal. Go."

I had cried so much already, I didn't feel as though I had any more tears left. It almost felt disrespectful *not* to cry, but emotional numbness was overtaking my body. I had trouble letting any words or tears flow. I slowly shifted to the right past Nicholas, Zachary, and Melissa to Makenah. Sweet, sweet Makenah. Her arms were at her side, slightly bent at the elbows—like a ballerina in first position—and she was dressed in her pretty pink Easter dress. She looked as if she were dancing.

"I love you, peanut butter cup. I shall always love you, Makenah. Dance for Jesus, Makenah. Don't stop. Keep on dancing."

I moved over to Alenah's frail little body. She appeared to be sleeping, dressed beautifully in a plain white outfit from China with a high collar. I still couldn't believe that she, too, was gone. It seemed as though we had just brought her home.

We never got to celebrate a birthday with her, or her first Halloween in the ladybug outfit Melissa had bought, or her first Thanksgiving, or her first Christmas. Oh, how I longed to have Alenah and all of them alive again so we could just enjoy life once more.

It seemed as though our children were finally coming into their own, into their element, and that life was finally getting a little simpler despite the challenges of our two special-needs children. And now all of their lives had been abruptly snuffed out.

"I love you, Alenah," I said to her. "Thank you for coming into our lives, sweet pea. Enjoy heaven with your mommy, your brothers, and your sissy."

There was one more thing I needed to do. I gently pinned delicate lace ribbons with the letters *SHMILY* on them to each member of my family: the two blue ribbons on my sons, the two pink ones on my daughters, and the ivory ribbon on my wife. The ribbons contained my last "letter" to them. "SHMILY" was a game Melissa and I learned in a book by Dr. and Mrs. James Dobson titled *Night Light*.[1] Makenah eventually joined in too.

One person would write the letters *SHMILY* on anything and hide it—like on a slip of paper stuffed in a shoe or in a pillowcase or written on the shower wall with shaving cream. Once hidden, it was the other person's turn to find it, like a treasure hunt that sometimes lasted days at a time. Once found, it was that person's turn to hide it and return the favor. It was just a fun little game that simply reinforced what we already knew so well.

SHMILY: "See How Much I Love You."

Now, with these five ribbons, it was my last turn. It would be my final message to accompany each of them to the grave and into eternity. I was the last one to "hide" the note.

Melissa and I had traveled halfway around the world to China and back without incident, only to have our family wiped out on a weekend trip to Wichita. Six eternal days after that terrible night, we were all together again in one room—but I was the only one still breathing, the only one remaining to wonder what went wrong.

Did we do the right things in the van? Should we have gotten out? Should I not have kicked out the window? Did we do everything humanly possible that we could have? How could I possibly ever face this cruel reality every morning? How could I live with this—with myself—with the harsh reality that I survived and the rest of my family didn't—and I couldn't save them? Did we make the right decisions in those last few minutes?

These questions would remain with me for weeks, months, perhaps even years to come. I had to remember the words of Dennis, my boss, on Sunday: "Robert, this is no time for should have, would have, or could have." He was right, but that would be easier said than done.

I walked to the back of the room and through the double doors. I needed to help my relatives and friends through the ordeal of this visitation. Even though they came in part to console me, I found myself consoling them. The best way I found to cope was to help others who hadn't yet tasted this bitter grief.

It was as if my misery was being turned into a ministry. By focusing outwardly on the needs of others rather than inwardly on my own pity or grief, I could heal much more quickly and completely. Like steam spewing out of a teakettle, I released my sorrow through the act of caring for others. I knew I had to pour myself out, or else I might drown in the well of my own tears.

Grandma Liz placed the handmade quilt she had just finished onto Alenah so that it would go to the grave with her. It was an important point of closure for her, knowing that she had now given each of my four children a handmade quilt.

Some of my nieces placed handwritten notes inside each casket. Nearly every one brought a smile to my face. One note in Nicholas's casket read, "I don't think they allow guns in heaven," referring to the plastic firearms at his sides in their holsters. Others placed little stuffed animals, toy figures, scarves, and even little Ghirardelli chocolate Squares in the caskets. Each article represented a point of connection and a point of release.

Some of my relatives withdrew to folding chairs in the room and wept. Others stared into space. Still others simply knelt and prayed. Several hours of intense grieving passed, and then it was time to leave. We drove home and gravitated toward the food. We needed nourishment and sustenance.

We also needed to lift our spirits somehow.

For generations, music has been a centerpiece for each side of my family. It has been life in our veins. We needed to infuse that life into our souls now more than ever. I was drawn to the piano in the living room. I needed to rest my ears from the chorus of audible grief all around me, and rest my voice from consoling others. I needed to play the piano and remain silent for a while. My fingers struggled to find their way across the keys. I meandered a bit and then played some old hymns, some worship songs, and some instrumental pieces I had written for my children.

My living room started filling with people on the floor, the sofa, the chairs, and the bed. Then my Aunt Ruthie from Boston, followed by Mom, Dad, Janet, and Kirk, gathered right around the piano. They started requesting various songs, but not sad dirges or tearful laments. We sang uplifting songs.

It was reminiscent of old times during Thanksgiving and Christmas with the relatives. Thank God for His gift of music in our lives. It was the balm we needed to salve the wounds in our souls. To anyone else passing by, it might have appeared completely irreverent and disrespectful for us to be engaged in festive melodies at such a time as this. But we needed to escape in a way that has always provided healing and renewal for our family. In a way, it also celebrated the lives of my wife and children, for this was the music they sang and danced to many nights before bedtime.

That pocket of music on Friday night served a valuable purpose. It was as if we all came up for air. We needed a chance to brace ourselves for tomorrow . . . the day I would bury my family.

26

One Last Good-bye

I woke up Saturday in Makenah's bed, disoriented and in a daze. I saw her birthday butterflies dangling from the ceiling. For a moment, I thought that I had drifted to sleep while putting Makenah to bed the night before, and perhaps she had already slipped out of bed and gone downstairs to watch Saturday-morning cartoons.

Then it hit me.

Once again, reality set in, and it dawned on me why I was here alone. I realized what I had to face this day: I would see Makenah and the rest of my children one last time, but in caskets at the church. I would never see Melissa's smile again on this earth.

I rolled out of bed and, out of force of habit, knelt in prayer.

"Good morning, Father. I come to You in the name of Jesus. I praise You and thank You for this beautiful day and all You have blessed us with . . ."

These words normally rolled off my tongue smoothly, from years of repetition, but this morning I could barely get the words out without breaking down in tears. How could I possibly call this a "beautiful day"? How could I still call myself "blessed"?

I opened my heart and did the only thing I could do. I honestly spilled out my grief, my doubts, my pain before the Lord.

"Dear God, I don't understand any of this. Nothing makes any sense anymore. All I know is that I can't make it through today without You. I need Your strength, because I have none left. All of mine is gone. Every ounce is drained. All I must face today is far too great for any mortal to bear. Please, Daddy, be the strength in my life. There's no way I can humanly get through this day on my own. It's all too much."

I knelt in silence for a few moments.

"Thank You, Lord. I still have to say 'Thank You' for all You've blessed me with over my life, for the years I had with Melissa and our kids. I'm thankful for another day closer to seeing You and my family in heaven. I still love You, Lord. I made it through a grueling day yesterday by trusting You. So, I will trust You for another day again."

I did my best to get ready. We took the 10-minute ride to the church. I had walked into this sanctuary many times over the past six years, usually with several children in tow. I had seen it decorated for many different seasons of the year. But I had never laid eyes on anything quite like this.

The altar and front area were flanked and overflowing with flower arrangements. Each one had its own unique design and beauty. The backdrop of flowers provided a bittersweet contrast to the somber view of five caskets on display in front of them.

Each casket had an easel next to it with memorabilia pinned to a foam core board: toothbrushes, pictures, boots, purses, swimsuits, dolls, ballet slippers, fans from China, toys, and stuffed animals. Scattered on the floor were larger backyard toys: a tricycle, a red Radio Flyer wagon, a big bouncy ball, and so on.

This was where we worshiped. Yet, just as Abraham had to lay down his son, Isaac, on an altar to God, this was where I had to lay down my entire family and not withhold them from Him. Abraham had waited one hundred years of his life for his beloved son. Then God asked for him back. I had worked what seemed to be my entire adult life to nurture a large, vibrant, thriving family. Now God had asked for them back.

If Abraham could do it, then so could I. If Job could fall to his knees and worship God after losing all 10 of his children, then so could I. Their example of faith inspired me as I faced this moment.

Melissa's casket was positioned in the center. She was the rock—the anchor of them all. Because of her appearance, Melissa's casket was now closed and had a bouquet of flowers and an angel figurine on top. The other four caskets were open. All of my children looked angelic, just as they had the night before at the private viewing.

We had arrived at the church around 8:15 A.M. The two-hour public viewing was scheduled to begin at 9:00 A.M. However, as soon as I entered the church, people started lining up to express their condolences.

People from all dimensions of our lives came by—our church, our children's schools, Zachary's therapists, Makenah's dance class, our children's Kindermusik class, our adoption agency, Melissa's MOPS (Mothers of Preschoolers) prayer group, my work associates, Melissa's babysitting co-op, Melissa's book-business friends at Usborne, and even many people I had never met—people who just felt connected and vested in my family's tragedy in some way.

As people came through the line and shook hands with my parents, Mom and Dad gently tugged them forward to help keep the line moving. The line grew and grew until it wound through the sanctuary and out the back door. More than 700 people passed through the sanctuary to see and pay tribute to my family one last time.

At one point, my brother Paul leaned over to me and said, "Robert, look at that!" The bright morning sun was shining into the church from the eastern sky, through the stained-glass windows depicting Jesus' second coming. The yellow beams were shining directly onto Alenah's casket and illuminating a small portion of her olive skin. It was remarkable.

It was as if God was reminding us of His promise of the resurrection, of His second coming, and of the ultimate hope in glory we have through Jesus. It felt to me as if God was trying to impress upon us, "Don't fret. Don't cry. Don't be afraid. This separation is very short and temporary. Before long, you will all be reunited in unspeakable joy."

That beam of light was a ray of hope and reassurance to keep our focus on eternal things, not on the overwhelming sadness in our midst. It felt as if God had reached down from heaven, through the windows, and given me a hug.

The procession of people hadn't eased when Nevin came to me just before 11:00 A.M. and said, "It's time, Robert." With his assistants, Nevin began directing the people in line to their seats.

It still seemed impossible. How could this be? I didn't want Nevin to close the lids on the caskets. I didn't want him to shut the door on my children—on my world—on my life. I didn't want to start a new life all over again. I didn't want to *have* to do this. *It wasn't supposed to be this way! It wasn't supposed to end like this!*

And yet, I had no choice. Nevin led my immediate family and Melissa's relatives out of the sanctuary and into the small chapel at the far end of the church. As he did, his helpers were closing and sealing the caskets back in the main sanctuary—in front of all 700 people. When they went to close Alenah's casket, the lid slipped and slammed shut with a sudden, thundering thud. A hush fell over the crowd as all eyes turned to her casket. The sound seemed to bring home the harsh finality of death.

Pastor Jerls gave us some final instructions in the small chapel and led us in prayer before we quietly proceeded back to the main sanctuary.

The funeral for my family was about to begin.

Pastor Jerls and I went to the center of the altar while the others took their seats in the front row. I approached the keyboard and microphone, where I wanted to use music to pierce the despair filling the room. Many have wondered how I could stand and speak any words, much less sing and play the piano, at my own family's funeral. Unless you are a fellow musician, it is difficult to explain. Music is how I express myself. My music was my tears.

I began with the last song I had composed while my family was still alive, something I had written just months before the flood. It seemed appropriate to set the tone of the service and to offer a balm to everyone's spirits. The lyrics to the song were almost prophetic, as if the Holy Spirit had inspired them for just this moment.

"There Is Peace"
© Robert T. Rogers, 2003

Do not be anxious, Do not be afraid
I go before you, I'm with you always
When all is said and done
When you've done all you can
It's time to let go, and let God . . .
There is peace. There is peace.

When I give control to You.
There is peace. There is peace.
Peace in the arms of God.

Pastor Jerls then opened the service with comforting words from the Book of Isaiah. This was the same passage of Scripture that Chaplain John Glennon had shared with me at Newman Memorial Hospital right after I had identified my children:

The good men perish; the godly die before their time and
no one seems to care or wonder why. No one seems to realize that God is taking them away from evil days ahead. For
the godly who die shall rest in peace. (57:1–2, TLB)

Those words were a comfort to me because they are one of the few places in Scripture that attempts to answer the question, "Why, God?"

After Pastor Jerls finished, it was my turn to speak. I first turned our thoughts to Melissa. With the microphone in one hand, I paced the platform and spoke freely from my heart about her, looking down upon her closed casket. I had not prepared any notes. I didn't need any. She was the love of my life. I could talk about her for hours. I spoke about how we met and all we had endured through- out our 13 and a half years of knowing each other—especially how she continued to love a man like me, even when my meticulous engineering side was annoying and difficult to cope with. I proudly declared my faithful love and devotion to her throughout our mar- riage, as I did on our wedding day at the front of a church and in front of a crowd much like this.

I made my way to the first pew and listened as several others eulogized Melissa as a daughter, a sister, a mother, and a friend.

After we had painted a beautiful, telling tribute to Melissa, Pastor Jerls read several verses from Psalm 139, concluding with verse 16: "Your eyes saw my unformed body. All the days ordained for me were written in your book before one of them came to be."

That verse spoke volumes to me. It said that God knew about the flash flood and knew my family would drown on August 30, 2003, long before they were ever born. I was comforted as I recognized that as premature as their deaths seemed, my wife and children had done everything on this earth they were supposed to. Even little Alenah at 21 months had lived a full life and affected many people.

Pastor Jerls then read Psalm 23 aloud. As I listened, bittersweet emotions struck me like waves. I had lost my family, and yet I could sense God's strength and peace sustaining me. His response wasn't automatic: I had to yield my bitterness and anger, my inclination to hold a grudge against Him. I had to surrender and let go to receive God's grace, but His grace filled me. I could indeed do all things through Christ who was giving me strength, moment by moment, just when I needed it in my darkest hours.

It was not by my might or my power but by God's comforting Holy Spirit that I was able to get through that torturous week, plus all that still awaited me. Because of His amazing grace and peace, I could honestly profess, "It is well with my soul." Janet, Kirk, and I sang that hymn together at the funeral. How many times since Spafford wrote it in the 1870s has that song been sung by people who can identify so deeply with the words? After pausing for several seconds, Pastor Jerls approached the microphone and shared the verses from the Book of Romans that he had spoken at the flood site on Tuesday after I identified Melissa:

And we know that all that happens to us is working for
our good if we love God and are fitting into his plans. . . .
Our fears for today, our worries about tomorrow, or where
we are—high above the sky, or in the deepest ocean—
nothing will ever be able to separate us from the love of
God demonstrated by our Lord Jesus Christ when he died
for us. (8:28, 38–39, TLB)

As the funeral service drew to a close, the heaviness hovering
over the crowd seemed to lift. The service blossomed into a joyful
celebration of life rather than a sad memorial of death.

Pastor Jerls read some final scriptures from 1 Thessalonians
4:13–18 about Christ's second coming. It was time to offer God's
rest, God's peace, and eternal life to everyone there. The life and
death before our eyes put everything in clear perspective: At the end
of the day, when all is said and done, what one thing is really going
to last in life? What is really worth living for?

Pastor Jerls asked everyone to bow their heads and close their
eyes. "If today were your last day," he asked, "would you go to
heaven?" He invited them to raise their hands if they weren't sure.
Hands went up all across the room. Then he acknowledged their
hands and led them in a simple prayer to commit their hearts completely to Christ.

To me, this was the most important part of the entire service.
Even if only one life was changed as a result, what greater good could
have come out of my family's deaths?

In keeping with the upbeat spirit of hope and joy of eternal life
in the room, Pastor Jerls then began describing how my family and
I used to sing a fun song at night before bedtime. We finished the

service and exited the sanctuary singing the lighthearted song "A Bushel and a Peck" as a tribute to my family and a challenge to us to remain upbeat, to keep singing, and to keep living.

It was heartening to have this cheerful tune dancing in our minds as we left the service. My relatives and I followed the pastor and the funeral procession out of the sanctuary and toward the limousines as people hugged me at every opportunity.

It was time to bury my family.

27

Balloons for Heaven

B lue skies and abundant sunshine greeted us as we stepped outside, and the sun's warmth on my skin felt good. After the two-hour funeral service on top of nearly three hours of public visitation, I needed that.

Nevin ushered me into the head limousine, along with my parents and Melissa's parents. The five hearses pulled out of the church parking lot first, and then we followed, along with four other black limousines carrying my siblings and other close friends and relatives. An entourage of nearly 15 police officers riding motorcycles escorted us. I later learned that these police officers represented four different police departments from neighboring cities. They were all generously volunteering their time and had arrived early to coordinate radio signals and practice the entire funeral-procession route.

Liberty and the surrounding communities had been reading, seeing, and hearing about this tragedy for seven straight days. Now they were experiencing it firsthand.

As we crossed intersections, with the police officers blocking traffic from all directions, I noticed mothers with tears streaming down their cheeks as they waited with their families in minivans. I saw teenagers at a Saturday-afternoon carwash fund-raiser, stopped in their tracks, with dripping sponges in their hands and their mouths open as they watched the mournful parade stretch out before their eyes.

I saw parents and children on ball fields stop what they were doing, paralyzed by such a dramatic sight. I saw older gentlemen respectfully place their hats over their chests, tears trickling down their faces. Others were saluting. Some placed their right hands over their hearts. It seemed as if we were passing by in slow motion, and I was able to zoom in and focus on every face, perceiving every emotion that poured out.

At one point, I caught sight of the procession of hearses through the windshield. The massive motorcade was stunning. I was honored, proud, and humbled all at once. The very sight of such an intense scene not only provoked powerful emotions within me but also left a noticeable impact on those watching. I could see how, even now, God was using this tragedy to touch and inspire others.

Nevin had intentionally mapped out the path to the cemetery to pass in front of our home on Liberty Drive. As I saw our house approaching through the front window, I felt a pain in the pit of my stomach. I had approached our home hundreds of times on my way back from work over the past six years, eagerly anticipating a warm homecoming. I had gone to Wichita every three weeks and returned home each time, eager to kiss Melissa and hug my kids. We had traveled all the way to China and back safely.

But my family never made it home from the trip to Wichita the previous Saturday—until now. I felt a strange sense of completion and closure. I was grateful to Nevin for routing the funeral procession in front of my home. It meant a great deal to me. We passed through downtown Liberty and eventually pulled into Glenridge Cemetery.

A large white tent had been erected over the grave sites. One by one, my siblings carried all five caskets from the hearses to the graves. My boss, Dennis, and a few others helped. I couldn't cry. I could barely move. All I could do was watch. As the last casket was put in place, side by side with the others, Pastor Jerls began with a prayer and Scripture reading. We all gathered under the tent, behind the caskets. The committal ceremony was brief.

We concluded with the hymn "We Are Standing on Holy Ground." I quietly sang it along with sign-language motions I had learned years before. As we reached the line "and I know that there are angels all around," I sensed tingles all about me.[1] It was as if Melissa and our children were standing alongside us in spirit as part of the great cloud of heavenly witnesses (Hebrews 12:1). We sang that hymn in church nearly every Sunday for the past six years. We learned it in sign language to help Zachary. But this time, it meant more to me than ever before. This indeed felt like holy ground.

After the ceremony, my nieces and nephews handed out small containers of bubbles to everyone. The bubbles were playful, much like our kids. They reminded us of children, celebrations, parties, and happy times. And yet the lifetime of each bubble was so terribly brief—lasting only a few seconds before it burst into thin air—reminding us of the brevity of life.

I leaned over and kissed the caskets and gave my final blessing to each one. Then I stepped out into a clearing and took hold of five balloons that my brother George had brought for me. They were simple metallic Mylar balloons with no design or message on them, and they reflected the glistening sun. Each one represented a soul of my family member. One by one, I released them to heaven.

With each one, I slowly let go of the base of the balloon and then allowed the entire length of the long tail to slip through my fingers. I tried to hold on to each last little shred of thread before relinquishing it to the wind. Each one was excruciating as I pondered each full life before letting go: 13 and a half years with Melissa, more than eight years with Makenah, almost six years with Zachary, nearly four years with Nicholas, and only eight short months with Alenah.

All five balloons drifted northeast and formed a line up toward heaven. They glistened beautifully in the sun against the backdrop of a clear sky. Melissa's balloon led the way to heaven—much as I imagined she must have led them all to heaven the week before. Alenah's balloon was drifting off course.

Jere blurted out, "Well, there goes Alenah, doing her own thing—like always!" We all got a good chuckle out of that comment.

We stood there staring up to heaven, tears streaming down our faces. We hung on until the final glimmer of balloons faded into the blue sky. Then we looked around at one another, trying to figure out what to do next.

It was all over. All I could mutter was, "It is finished."

We headed silently back to church, where a reception was awaiting us. I sat at a large table with my friends and, for the first time, felt the stark reality of being lonely. I wasn't alone, but I was lonely. I was lonely for my family. I was longing for the days when I had three kids in my lap, and Melissa and Makenah were gathering plates of food from the buffet for everyone. I felt out of my element. I felt off balance, limping along, as if I didn't belong in this setting without them. It just didn't feel right.

Shortly after we arrived home, I headed straight for bed. I was wiped out and just needed to rest. I chose the boys' room and curled up on Zachary's bed. Janet came and knelt on the floor by my side.

As I lay in Zachary's bed in a fetal position, my world suddenly came crashing down.

I released the depth of grief that had been welling up all week, and especially that day—my own grief plus the grief I carried from everyone who tried to console me. I cried out in vain, "Why God? Why? I loved the family I had!"

Janet just gripped my hand. I felt the abject loneliness and the looming aloneness. I realized that everything Melissa and I had done to raise a loving family was gone. Completely gone. As that reality hit me, I panicked.

"What do I do? Where do I go? How do I move on?"

The tears just wouldn't stop. The pain in the pit of my stomach would not cease. All I could do was cry myself to sleep.

A few hours later, I woke and stumbled downstairs. I felt a measure of relief after that cleansing cry and a much-needed rest.

I found my sister Anne. As we passed through the laundry room with Janet, we were drawn to the calendar hanging on the door to the cleaning supplies. It was a 12-month calendar Makenah had made more than a year before in her first-grade class. It was still turned to the month of August. The calendar resembled a coloring book, with 12 blank outlines to color. Each one matched the monthly season or holiday: fireworks in July, a snowman in December, a valentine in February, and so on. On each month, Makenah had carefully colored in the picture and added extra creativity.

As we turned the page to September, we couldn't believe our eyes. We noticed that the original picture was an outline of a school bus with a woman driving and two boys and a girl on board. Makenah had colored the bus yellow. But she had also added several things: green grass, green bushes, a blue sky, a house with a chimney (much like ours), and a traffic signal colored red.

Then, of all things, right next to where she printed her name, she drew a picture of herself flying up to heaven—with a great big smile on her face! She portrayed herself floating above the bus with her feet off the ground, holding six balloons. It was the only month of the entire year that she had added a person to the existing picture. The symbolism was both deeply comforting and uncanny.

Makenah was holding six balloons. Six people died the night of the flood: Al Larsen plus my family. I had released balloons to heaven at the cemetery only a few hours earlier. The stoplight was red, as if that was the end of the line for the bus—our van. A woman was driving the bus, just as Melissa had been driving our van when we hit the flash flood. A girl and two boys were still in the bus, just as Zachary, Nicholas, and Alenah were still strapped in their car seats when they found the van. Plus, I was nowhere in the picture—only the five of them were shown.

"Robert, stay right there!" Janet exclaimed. She ran to the dining room where boxes of pictures were stacked on the table. All week long, my siblings had been assembling scrapbooks using my family pictures.

Earlier in the week, Janet and Kirk had taken the last two rolls of film that were found in the van wreckage—one in a plastic canister, and the other still in the camera—to a special photo lab. The photo lab was able to salvage most of the pictures, including priceless pictures from Makenah's birthday just three weeks earlier, a picture of all four children eating Popsicles on our front porch step, and a nearly perfect family picture taken at the wedding reception—with all four kids looking at the camera! It was our last family picture ever taken, just hours before the flash flood.

One picture in particular caught Janet's attention now. She ran back to Anne and me with it pinched between her fingers, shouting, "You guys! Look! Look!"

She placed it next to Makenah's September calendar picture so

we could see them side by side. We could barely believe our eyes.
Janet held up the last picture taken of our children, just outside the
church after the wedding. The bride and groom had driven away
from the reception, leaving all the balloons that we had stuffed into
their car floating and bouncing around on the pavement under the
protection of the valet car covering. While our children and their
cousins were playing with the balloons, we snapped a picture of
them holding the balloons.

All four kids were standing on a picnic bench next to each other
in a row. Zachary, in his bare feet, was holding on to the back of the
bench with both hands. Alenah was holding a blue balloon and was
looking up at Makenah. Nicholas was sporting a big smile and holding an orange balloon. Makenah was holding a pink balloon in one
hand and an orange balloon in the other, with both arms fully
extended up toward heaven, smiling so wide she could have eaten a
banana sideways. She looked as happy as could be—just like in the
calendar picture she had drawn more than a year earlier, with the balloons in her hands. And behind Makenah in the photo was a stoplight, situated the same way as the one she intentionally added to her
calendar.

Now, I've never been superstitious, but I also don't believe in
coincidences. I believe in "God-incidences." To me, this was no accident. These two pictures side by side were nothing short of a gift
from God. Makenah's calendar was truly prophetic. I believe that
God entered the heart and mind of my oldest daughter in 2002
when she was only seven years old to plant a message for her daddy
to read on September 6, 2003, as if to say, "I am fine. We all went
to heaven and are as happy as can be. You don't need to cry any
longer, Daddy."

God had not failed me. I felt as though He had just wrapped His big daddy-arms around me and reminded me, "It's all right, Robert. I divinely ordained this event. I knew about this before you were born. Your family is fine and safe with Me in heaven—where there are no tears, no sadness, and no dying."

I no longer felt disappointed with God. My trust was refreshed and emboldened. I realized that when I fully trust God's plan, I will never be disappointed. I may *feel* disappointed when my trust is tested, but I don't have to constantly *be* disappointed because I know that God and all His plans for me are still good (Jeremiah 29:11). He truly is the God of all comfort.

Thank You, Jesus, for Makenah's gift, I prayed. *Thank you, Makenah, for following the inspiration to draw such a prophetic picture.*

Because of her picture and our children's last photo, I was able to sleep peacefully that night.

28

Empty

I awoke on Sunday with an empty heart in an empty bed in an empty room in my empty home.

I was empty.

In the aftermath of the worst week of my life, I was utterly drained of all strength. I wanted to stay in bed for the rest of my life. I didn't want to move. I felt paralyzed, as if my legs were wedged in concrete. I could have stayed there until I withered away into nothing. Part of me wanted to.

It was enormously difficult for me to face another day—alone. But I knew that God wanted me to keep living, to be productive with my life, and to do good things for Him. So I chose to get up. Only I couldn't muster the strength on my own. Again, the scriptures I learned years ago resounded in my ears: "My grace is sufficient for you, for my power is made perfect in weakness" (2 Corinthians 12:9), and "I can do all things through Christ who strengthens me" (Philippians 4:13, NKJV).

God's words gave me the hope and the strength to face one more minute of one more day. I realized that something was going to fill me up—either something worldly or something godly. I chose to be filled by God.

I felt so cocooned in God's lap that I didn't want to dishonor Him. The part of me that had always worked hard to please my teachers and my parents as a child now wanted to please my heavenly Father. I wanted my life to be a living tribute to my family.

On that awful Sunday morning, I found the strength to go on. I dressed and went to church, where most of my relatives had gathered for a final service together before flying home. As was my custom, I arrived 30 minutes before the 10:00 A.M. service to play instrumental prelude music as the people filed into the sanctuary. Many people were bewildered to see me there—fully functioning and coherent, much less making music again. After all, I had buried my family just the day before.

But I had to face the pain of a new day and embrace it as my own. I believed that my suffering was sacred and somehow ordained by God. I intentionally played uplifting and upbeat songs, as if to spite the devil and say, "You're *not* going to steal my joy. You can't take that away from me."

Jesus assured us that "you will weep and mourn. . . . You will grieve, but your grief will turn to joy" (John 16:20), and "Weeping may endure for a night, but joy comes in the morning" (Psalm 30:5, NKJV). So I broke into a joyful tune that I had learned years earlier with Ron Kenoly called "Mourning into Dancing." Taking courage and adopting an attitude of thanksgiving and worship were terrifying. It's one of the hardest choices I ever made. But what I discovered amazed me: I found complete joy and contentment.

As I worshiped God on the keyboard and soon made my way down to the pew to sing along with the congregation, I experienced a oneness with God like never before. I started crying profusely. I could barely utter decipherable words. And yet I didn't need to. My tears were a form of worship too.

No words could describe my level of anguish, but words could not describe my level of peace, either. This was not denial. This was not an escape. My soul was at rest, fully alive and vibrant. It defied explanation or understanding. Rather than wallowing in my pity, I worshiped in God's presence. Once I did, I found that my worries and self-pity diminished dramatically. They didn't disappear, but they became significantly lighter.

It doesn't mean that every moment has been joyful or good. It doesn't mean that everything I have uttered has been positive or praiseworthy. I have messed up and fallen down plenty of times. I have sweet times and bitter times. I have extreme highs with God and devastating lows from grief. But I always come back to worship.

My worship was the kind of obedient sacrifice Abraham demonstrated when he went to the mountain to sacrifice his own son, Isaac. As a result of his unconditional obedience, the angel of the Lord declared, "Because you have done this and have not withheld your son, your only son, I will surely bless you" (Genesis 22:16–17).

It was the type of spontaneous worship Job offered after he lost all 10 of his children and still "fell to the ground in worship and said: '. . . The LORD gave and the LORD has taken away; may the name of the LORD be praised.' In all this, Job did not sin by charging God with wrongdoing" (Job 1:20–22). If Job didn't sin by what he said, I didn't want to either.

On that first Sunday after the funeral, I decided to make a point of worshiping daily, whether I was at home alone by the piano, in my car, or walking around the block.

After church, my family and I gathered many of the flowers and mementos from the memorial in my side yard. We tearfully said good-bye, and all of them went their separate ways. But my parents, my sister Anne, and Janet Hughes stayed for another week.

While they were still with me, my parents contacted St. James Church in Liberty and asked for advice on counseling. We set up an appointment with a licensed professional counselor in conjunction with lay ministers from the church's Stephens Ministries program. We met in a group session that week and began the lifelong journey of purging our wounds. Our counselor, Nancy, immediately gave us two rules to follow:

1. Don't hurt yourself.

2. Don't hurt anyone else.

She also gave us freedom to release our feelings of anger, loss, and betrayal—whether creatively through writing, composing, singing, or painting, or even destructively, such as slamming the kitchen cabinets or breaking dinner plates—provided we didn't hurt anyone in the process. She also urged me not to make any major life decisions for at least a year.

Before we left our first session, Nancy recommended a personal psychotherapist who specializes in trauma. I also called Focus on the Family and spoke at length with a member of the professional staff in their counseling department, who offered words of comfort and recommended several professional counselors near where I lived.

I began personal counseling right away. From the start, it was extremely positive and helpful. My counselor helped me navigate the rough seas of grief. The process was like slowly peeling an onion. Each layer made me cry, but week by week, with each successive counseling session, we peeled away another coating of grief. The process was tremendously cleansing.

Counseling validated my feelings as acceptable and normal. It helped me recognize that I wasn't crazy or disconnected from my heart. My counselor picked up on common threads and themes that I unknowingly mentioned from week to week, such as tumbling in the water after kicking out the window. We worked through those recurring themes and eventually defused them. She also helped with my feelings of failure and guilt.

It was important to me that my parents were by my side as this journey of healing and understanding began. Their presence was calming to me. They were a solid rock of faith, just as they have been my entire life.

I returned to work a few weeks after the funeral, but it felt pointless.

My whole reason for being an electrical engineer was to support my family. With Melissa and our children gone, my reason for working was gone too. I lost all purpose and motivation. I was just going through the motions. I had no qualms over resigning, because my career never defined me. By living frugally and simply, I could resign from my job and give myself the time I needed to adjust to the changes in my life.

I needed to discover the destiny for which God had saved me. Over the ages, many great men ventured into the wilderness before their life's calling began. Moses watched sheep for 40 years before leading the Israelites out of Egypt. Joseph resourcefully used his time in prison until Pharaoh promoted him to second in command over all of Egypt. Jesus spent 40 days in the desert before formally beginning His ministry. Whatever God wanted me to do with the rest of my life, I sensed I needed to retreat from the world to discover it.

Before I could retreat, however, I would have to step forward. I was invited to go to New York to appear on ABC's *Good Morning America* with Diane Sawyer and on CNN's *American Morning* with Soledad O'Brien. I agreed to the interviews because I hoped to inspire others to cherish their families and one another. I wanted to be a beacon of hope to those who were hurting.

I asked my father to accompany me for emotional support. My appearance on *Good Morning America* was scheduled for the morning after our arrival. Amazingly, I wasn't nervous at all. It seemed that I had lost all earthly fear in the flood. I figured I was going to have a quiet conversation with Diane Sawyer. They led us to the set, and my father looked on from the side of the room. They seated me in a comfortable chair on the opposite side of the set from the morning headline news.

The set was remarkably hushed. I felt as if I were in someone's living room. Then, just after the 8:00 A.M. news headlines with Robin Roberts, Diane came over and greeted me with a warm embrace. We sat and waited for the cue and then started talking. Many around the country were praying along with me that God would pour out all the right words from my mouth. Like Moses, I prayed that God would speak to me and put the words in my mouth, and teach me what to do (Exodus 4:15).

Diane asked me thoughtful questions and we shared a very quiet conversation. At one point, I started talking about identifying my children, and I choked up. I could see tears well up in Diane's eyes as well, but she kept her composure as a consummate professional. It was a very emotional moment. After the seven-minute segment, she embraced me again and asked me to make sure I sought counseling. I assured her that I had already begun.

I sensed that many people thought I had completely lost it, that I was in complete denial. But I hadn't lost it. I found it: the Way, the Truth, and the Life. I already knew the Truth, and He set me free. My faith in Jesus Christ defused the sting of death and infused the hope of life. The grief certainly still stings at times, but the hope of eternal life is far greater and was fully able to carry me through the funeral, the burial, and all the trials I've experienced since. God freed me from all fear, and my face radiated His joy.

Death had no power over me because it had no power over Christ, and Christ lives within me. The same Spirit that raised Jesus from the dead dwells in me—and all Christians. That's why the death of my family didn't kill or cripple me. Without my faith, I would have died too. I've seen people for whom the death of a loved one became a fatal blow for them as well. But it doesn't have to be that way—not with an abiding faith and knowledge of the essence of Christ. We have the ultimate hope of Christ for eternity.

Just after the interview concluded, Charles Gibson came over and shook my hand. He was in a hurry to head downstairs for the next segment, but it seemed that he went out of his way to introduce himself. I was honored by how kindly and graciously they both treated us.

We left the building and started walking down 44th Street. Friends who saw the interview immediately started calling my cell phone. They were blown away by the words that had come out of my mouth. The Holy Spirit had indeed given me words of hope, encouragement, and faith. It truly wasn't my doing.

While Dad and I were in New York, we briefly discussed the notion of taking a train trip. It felt like the perfect time and method for me to retrace some of my past and seek direction for the future.

Not long after I returned home to Liberty, I embarked on a three-week wilderness journey during which I would touch both coasts. Only minutes after boarding Amtrak's Southwest Chief, the rhythm and gentle rocking of the train lulled me to sleep. I awoke to the sunrise, startled by the sight of the beautiful southern Rockies. The orange and auburn colors of the fall blended seamlessly with the colors of the southwest states. The journey transported me to our humble beginnings in 1991, when Melissa and I married and drove through the Southwest to start our lives together in California.

I found the train to be extremely tranquil. It forced me to slow down, be still, and reflect. I was free from rush-hour traffic, turn signals, merging lanes, and any decisions about where to go. The steel rails already determined our course.

Along the journey, I was privileged to meet interesting people at my table in the dining car. Every meal became an opportunity to get to know new people. I met a fun and lighthearted elderly Jewish gentleman. He asked to know why I was traveling alone, and once I told him my story, his tone and demeanor changed. He grew quiet and then told me he would pray for me; he then rolled up his sleeve to show me his arm. I could see the serial number tattooed there—evidence of the time he had spent at a Nazi concentration camp. I was sitting next to a man who had faced death on a daily basis. What a story he had to tell. No wonder humor was so important to him.

All along the way, God put remarkable people in my path. I wasn't wearing my feelings on my sleeve, but often my family would just come up in conversation, and I'd tell my story. People would see my wedding ring or we'd share family photos, and they would ask further questions. Their responses were often same: shock, tears, disbelief, discomfort, and a desperate—often futile—search for reassuring words. I tried my best to console them. As we parted ways, each person was noticeably changed.

I didn't realize it at the time, but those conversations on the train were the first fruits of a blossoming ministry: I was witnessing the power of testimony as my family's story began changing people's lives. It was extraordinary to behold.

The train arrived in California amid heavy downpours. The sight and sound of the rain brought back horrific memories. I changed trains in Los Angeles to head south to San Diego to visit my dear friend Kay King, who was now a retired widow. I was her musical director for the Mini-Mummers in Cincinnati for 10 years. After a visit lasting several days, I boarded the train again and headed north to San Jose. Melissa and I had spent more than five years there, and it was where Makenah was born.

I rented a car and stayed with some old friends. I needed to touch the places Melissa and I had been—and process the fact that my life up to this point was now simply a collection of memories. I drove to the park where we had camped and hiked with Makenah in the backpack child carrier. I found the ranch near the coast where we had picked strawberries. I drove along the Pacific Coast Highway to Half Moon Bay. I parked near the beach and walked barefoot through the sand as I revisited where we had picnicked and played in the frigid Pacific Ocean. Makenah had winced the first time her feet touched the freezing ocean when she was just a few months old. My heart ached as I relived so many vivid memories.

I continued northward up Highway 1 into San Francisco and headed to Ghirardelli Square near Fisherman's Wharf. I found my way to the Ghirardelli chocolate shop and ordered chocolate ice cream, dipped in chocolate, and smothered in almonds, just the way Melissa loved it. I found the table for two by the window where we'd shared dessert numerous times.

Then I walked down to the wharf and peered out at the glistening Golden Gate Bridge as tears streamed down my cheeks and wind blew against my face. So many romantic dreams and memories started here and laid a foundation for our marriage. I still couldn't believe they were all gone.

Next, I hopped aboard a train and visited friends in Fresno and Sacramento, including Melissa's best friend, Eri. Then it was time to head east. I settled into a sleeper car aboard the California Zephyr. The train trudged slowly through tunnels from the gold-rush era, around gorgeous mountain bends, onward to Denver, and then to Chicago.

I had an extended layover in Chicago before my train continued to Washington, D.C., so I checked my bags and hit the windy streets. I walked up Michigan Avenue and reminisced about the gentle snow that had fallen on New Year's Eve when I brought Melissa here for our seventh anniversary. Along Lakeshore Drive, I thanked God for the visit our family had spent there over Memorial Day weekend, just three months before the flood. It had kicked off the best summer of our lives.

It hit me especially hard when I stood in front of the old water tower on Michigan Avenue just south of the John Hancock Center. Our family had taken a beautiful portrait there. My children's feet had touched the very pavement where I was standing. I felt a deep, somber connection to them. It hurt. And it healed.

I boarded my sleeper car on the Capitol Limited train and headed east to Washington. The radiant autumn colors of the Appalachian Mountains and Harpers Ferry were beautiful to behold as I wrote in my journal and began composing music. I rented a car in Washington and drove across the mighty Chesapeake Bay Bridge into Delaware for the three-hour drive to Rehoboth Beach. My parents had been going there every year for more than 40 years and had a few days left over from my Uncle Joe's time-share for me to use.

I had taken my family there in 1999 and again in 2001, and we built wonderful memories. I wanted to touch those places again—

and let them go. I rented a bike and rode up and down Route 1 to Bethany Beach and the mile-long boardwalk at Rehoboth. I walked, prayed, and reminisced along the shore and out on the jetties.

After driving back to Washington, D.C., I stayed with my brother George and his family for a few days. I walked around the city alone during the day, remembering the two times our family had visited here. We were honored to tour the White House just three months before 9/11. The Vietnam Veterans Memorial struck me especially hard this time as I touched the mortality of so many who laid down their lives for our country. I saw parents reach out to touch the name of their lost child.

Soon it was time to head home. I contemplated all the places I had visited over the past three weeks and was somber and pensive the entire ride. Upon my return to Liberty, each day became a matter of motivating myself to get out of bed and do worthwhile, constructive things with the time I had remaining on this earth.

I paid a visit to Janet and Kirk in Fort Wayne, Indiana. For several days, they took me in, nurtured me, and ministered to me. They knew me so well that they were even able to make me laugh from time to time. It felt so healing to laugh again with friends.

One afternoon, they took me to a charming place deep in the woods called the Quiet Corner. It was a restaurant designed as a large indoor gazebo, nestled among the trees, with rocking chairs and hiking trails outside and a piano and gift shop inside. Janet introduced me to the owners, Dick and Shirley, and we shared my story. The lunch crowd had already left, so we ordered some delicious soup and sandwiches to snack on as the owners and several employees pulled up chairs to listen in.

After I told my story, Janet encouraged me to play some of the songs I had recently composed. As the vivid emotions and memories of my experience were still extremely raw, I poured out my feelings through the music. After I finished singing, I noticed that our waitress, Inga, was wiping away tears. She seemed sincerely touched by my story and the music. When I got up from the piano, we gave each other a brief hug. Then as we were leaving, I thanked Dick and Shirley for their part in creating this special afternoon. The time shared with friends, amid such peaceful surroundings, was like healing oil for my spirit.

The weeks I spent on the train trip and the time I spent visiting old friends provided me with the comfort of people who cared about me and the opportunity to remember my beautiful family in solitude, processing what had happened and praying for direction about my future.

29

A Ministry Blossoms

I was still occasionally approached by various news media outlets for interviews, including another trip to New York to appear on *The Montel Williams Show*. There, I met Al Larsen's widow, Elizabeth. We chatted for a bit and recounted Al's last moments, his heroic efforts, and Melissa calling out his name in vain. We tightly embraced before saying good-bye. My parting words conveyed that I would forever be indebted to her for her husband's selfless and priceless effort to try to save my family.

A few weeks after I returned home from the train trip, a church in Parkville, Missouri, asked me to share my story and my faith at their Saturday-morning pancake breakfast. I gladly accepted.

I brought along poster-board pictures and a copy of Makenah's calendar. I presented some songs I had composed, but mainly I just spoke from my heart. I had never been trained to speak in front of others. I'm comfortable in front of a piano keyboard, not a microphone. The last thing I ever wanted was a ministry where I had to get up and speak. Yet afterward, the comments I heard over and over were "inspiring" and "compelling."

My words challenged people to transform their faith into something real. I called parents to love each other and cherish their children. My words drew people to the power of the cross of Jesus Christ. I was astonished at the effectiveness of a testimony—not *my* testimony but God's testimony of grace through my life. I was just the instrument He was using to display His power.

Word of mouth spread, and soon many other churches in the area invited me to speak. I met with several local pastors for prayer or just to talk over lunch and later spoke at their churches. It was all I could do to keep up with the requests. I never felt right asking for compensation to tell my story. Instead, the churches welcomed free-will offerings to help me continue presenting my story.

My sister Mary and her two daughters came to visit and help me celebrate Zachary and Alenah's birthdays in November, just three months after the flood. Mary baked two cakes, and we took them to the cemetery, sang "Happy Birthday," blew out the candles, and ate a slice with some ice cream. I released two balloons and sent Zachary and Alenah my love, wishing them the best birthday party ever in heaven. As the balloons ascended, tears welled up in my eyes as I envisioned Zachary at age six and Alenah at age two. How I ached to celebrate just one of Alenah's birthdays with her here.

During Mary's visit, we spent an entire day scouring the flood site. We bundled up in windbreakers, sweatshirts, hats, and gloves. The air was bitter cold, and a light rain was falling. Because of the irregular terrain and tall grass, there were many items from our van still scattered around Jacob Creek. Also, as the water had continued to recede, more fragments from our van and personal items were uncovered.

We brought plastic bags and collected my family's belongings from along the riverbanks and creek bed: the van mirror, Melissa's skirt and blouse, Makenah's favorite "77" T-shirt and "Sweet Dreams" pillowcase, Zachary's tan shorts, Nicholas's blue pants, the red-white-and-blue polka-dot outfit Alenah had worn at the wedding, my suit pants, all three handmade quilts from Grandma Liz, the stroller, our stadium blanket, and the Paploo teddy bear that I had used as a pillow in the van. We even found an entire duffel bag and its contents strewn about. It belonged to Al Larsen, the man who had died trying to save us. We gathered it and made sure his widow, Elizabeth, received it.

After six difficult drenching hours covering more than four miles, we arrived back at the car and changed into dry clothes. It was a painfully therapeutic day. I had confronted my family's path of death from start to finish.

As a tribute to Melissa, I decided to finish painting and remodeling our bedroom. We had planned to apply the first coat of primer on the night we returned from the wedding in Wichita. We had just finished the drywall and were ready to start painting. Melissa had already picked out the deep blue paint color and the carpet. All the materials had been bought and paid for. It took five coats, but I finished on December 22. The next day, workers installed the carpet. The room was finished in time for Christmas. It was beautiful. Melissa would have loved it.

On Christmas Eve, I went out and bought a live tree. I decorated it sparsely, to represent the condition of my life. I built a fire in our brick fireplace, with my family's stockings hanging from the mantel. I intentionally spent Christmas Eve and Christmas morning alone at home. I just felt I needed to immerse myself in the moment in solitude.

I attended midnight Mass at St. James up the street and pictured our kids from the previous year's service there—yawning and snuggled in their jammies. For the first time since the flood, I lay in our bed that night in our newly remodeled bedroom, thinking of how we dreamed for years of sharing this moment together in our new room. I drifted off to sleep, drenched in tears.

I woke up Christmas morning, not quite sure what to do with myself. I wandered around the house, gravitated toward the piano, and composed a song. I visited the cemetery and brought along five helium-filled balloons. I carefully hand-selected each one and wrote a personal note with a marker. One by one, I released them to heaven—where I imagined my family receiving and reading the notes.

I visited Melissa's family in Kansas and wished them the best Christmas possible, given what had happened. Then I flew to Cincinnati to be with my parents. The three of us attended evening Mass at St. Lawrence Church in Price Hill on December 31, which was the very place and time that Melissa and I had married. We sat up near the front where Mom and Dad had sat during our wedding ceremony, and we were fighting back tears the entire service.

I then attended the Cincinnati Symphony Orchestra's New Year's Eve gala concert alone at the grand Music Hall. The symphony was magnificent, and the music was soothing and therapeutic. After the concert, I made my way to the Hilton in downtown Cincinnati where Melissa and I had spent our wedding night. As I entered room 2410, I was greeted by a plate of 12 chocolate-covered strawberries sprinkled with pristine powdered sugar, and a huge bottle of spring-water on ice. The manager evidently sent them up after my mother reserved the room and told him all about my reason for staying overnight. The 12 strawberries represented our 12th anniversary.

I brought with me a six-inch, round white-chocolate cake with raspberry filling made by the same bakery that had made our wedding cake. It was garnished with white chocolate swirls and strawberries—just the way Melissa loved it. Lastly, I toasted Melissa with a sip of Maui Blanc pineapple wine, which Melissa and I had bought in 1995, hoping to save it for a very special anniversary celebration someday. I felt it was important to open it on this New Year's Eve and toast Melissa, to honor our memories and nearly 12 years of marriage, and to say good-bye.

Some in my family thought I was out of my mind to do such a painful thing. But for me, I needed to immerse myself in every dimension of the moment so that I could properly release it. I looked through a scrapbook filled with photos of our wedding and honeymoon and relished every loving word Melissa had written alongside the pictures. I was so thankful that I was true to her in good times and in bad, in sickness and in health. And I vowed to still honor her and cherish the memory of her all the days of my life.

As a tribute to my family in heaven, I vowed to keep myself pure while I waited to marry again—if and when it was God's will. As the glistening ball over Times Square descended and Dick Clark rang in the New Year, I sipped some bitter pineapple wine and thanked Melissa for all of our cherished years together. I dozed off around 2:30 A.M., thinking of our wedding night 12 years earlier.

The next morning, I woke up refreshed and felt the dawn of a new season of my life. I wrote in the last page of the journal we had intended to give to our children.

Thursday January 1, 2004

Melissa—I shall always love you and always miss you. I shall always treasure our time, our memories, our love, and most of all, our family together. Nothing and no one can ever replace you. . . . And so, as I turn to the last page of this journal of

memories, it's time for me to turn the final page on the chap-
ter of our lives. My book is not complete yet. I have more chap-
ters to fill, and I know you want me to fill them as we did
ours—with a smile on my face and making blessed and abun-
dant memories. . . . Thank you for making so many of my
dreams come true. I now release you into heaven—into our
Father's hands. I let you go. I surrender you. I submit com-
pletely to God's perfect will for my life. As I have prayed every
day—I'm willing and available to be obedient to God. . . .
Until we meet again, I love you.—Robert

That was the most difficult New Year's Eve I ever experienced. It was intense surgery. It hurt. And it healed.

I returned home and resumed work on my Master of Business Administration degree. I also accepted several more invitations to speak to groups about my family and the flood. Since I had memorized and recited Psalm 112 nearly every day, and since we often prayed over our children that they would be "mighty in the land" (verse 2), it became my anthem: a tribute to my children's mighty testimony across the earth, and a challenge to others to be mighty children of God who effectively impact God's kingdom across this land.

Mighty in the Land Ministry grew, and I enlisted the help of others with the Web site, logo, and scheduling. Once it became apparent that God was growing this ministry beyond my capabilities, I registered it as a nonprofit charity with the IRS, rented a cubicle for an office, hired an assistant, and enlisted a seven-member national board of directors to oversee the ministry and hold us accountable.

In June of 2004, I joined more than 30 relatives for our annual family reunion at Rehoboth Beach, Delaware. It helped me to just be around them all day at the beach and talk through old memories.

In early July, I went on a seven-day cruise sponsored by Focus on the Family. I had felt a desire to get away for a while, and the cruise seemed like an answer to prayer: a safe environment where I could continue my journey of healing and remembrance. I met remarkable men and women of God along the way and was honored to share dinner one evening with Dr. Dobson and his family.

After the cruise ended, I recorded many of the songs I had composed from my grieving. I set up a home studio and often recorded in the middle of the night, when all was quiet and peaceful outside. When I told my story at churches and schools, many people asked how they could get a copy of my songs. I decided to make them available on CDs as a tribute to my family. I finished a piano instrumental CD titled *Instrument of Hope* and a vocal CD titled *Resurrection*. They arrived from the CD duplicator a week before the first anniversary of the flood.

To commemorate the anniversary, my family and I planned a series of events in Kansas City, Emporia, and Wichita to publicly thank those who had prayed for us and blessed us in so many ways over the past 12 months. We invited people to come to special church services, where I honored my family through pictures, scriptures, and music. I described many of the remarkable testimonies of God's power through people's lives since the flood.

My family and I also planned some private events to help our healing and closure. We visited the church where the wedding reception took place the day of the flood. I showed everyone where Makenah had lifted balloons to heaven—just hours before *she* went to heaven. We went to the ice cream shop where my family had shared our last treat together. I couldn't help thinking of Melissa. From our first ice-cream date at Friendly's to our last treat shared at Braum's, God encased our fairy-tale romance with bookends made of ice cream, filled with sweet memories in between.

We attended the Al Larsen memorial ceremony at the Matfield Green service area along the turnpike and paid tribute to the immense sacrifice of two men—Al Larsen and Ryan Lane—who rescued several people from the flood, put their own lives on the line, and showed the greatest love possible.

After the memorial service, we rented a bus to shuttle nearly 40 of us to the flood site at milepost 116 along I-35. On the bus, I sat next to Ryan, who had been nearly knocked off his feet and swept away by the rushing waters as he led one elderly man to safety on the night my family died. He was urging traffic in the southbound lanes of the turnpike to back away from the rising waters when the surge swept us away.

He apologized for not being able to save my family, but no apology was needed. He had laid his life on the line for us and done everything he possibly could, and I feel eternally indebted to him for his efforts.

The highway patrol escorted us and protected us from the traffic driving by. For 30 minutes, we gazed upon and touched Jacob Creek's still waters and the Flint Hills' green pastures. For me, this was sacred ground. I pounded five tall redwood crosses into the earth. Al Larsen's brother pounded in the sixth—one for each person who had died. The hammer blows echoed through the valley, and I thought of Psalm 23. The blows pierced my heart like a final nail in the coffin. Though it was excruciating, I felt a sense of closure, relief, and finality. After more prayers and more tears, we boarded the bus and returned to our cars, looking quietly upon the beautifully rolling hills.

I awoke to a light drizzle in Wichita on August 30, 2004. I was restless that morning, and my parents were still asleep in our hotel room. I quietly slipped out of bed and put on my sneakers to go for a walk. As I stepped outside into the light rain, I looked up and saw something amazing. The sun majestically pierced through an opening in the clouds as it rose in the eastern sky. To the west, a magnificent double rainbow filled the sky!

On this of all days, on the anniversary of the flood, Almighty God chose to display the sign of His promise that He would never forsake us—the promise He gave to Noah after the Great Flood.

30

God Is Still Good

L ife felt different after one year. It felt like the dawn of a new season. I finally felt comfortable removing my wedding ring, though my finger felt bare without it. I kept touching that spot with my thumb, expecting to find my ring. It took me a long time to adjust to a bare finger, and I still wasn't comfortable with the thought of dating again.

I didn't visit the cemetery as frequently, and when I did, the pain gradually lessened. I found that grieving is a uniquely individual experience—we grieve as differently as we look. I learned that I could separate the grief from the good memories. On birthdays and holidays, I gradually became able to celebrate my family's lives without breaking down in tears every time. I learned that it was indeed possible to move on with life and still never forget my family. And I took comfort in the fact that purging the past does not mean forgetting. It means releasing.

I have continued to accept invitations to talk about my family, the flood, and how I have been able to handle that devastating loss cupped in God's loving hands. But the testimony has become more about helping people grow closer to Him and their families and challenging them to live a life of no regrets. It's about helping people appreciate who and what they have, because life is so fragile and can end so suddenly.

The world received a reminder of that truth when the tsunami struck in the Indian Ocean in late December 2004. I was powerfully drawn to the televised images of the devastated coastlines and villages, where countless thousands of people were killed. I felt a natural connection with these people who had also lost their families in turbulent waters. The next month, I accepted an invitation to travel with Children of Promise International to the tsunami zone.

I ministered on the coastal mainland of India and on the Andaman and Nicobar islands. I brought balloons and bubbles and played with the children. A doctor and nurse on our team gave medical attention. We brought food and prayed with the people and, through an interpreter, led many to accept Jesus as their personal Savior. They expressed their lost hope in their Hindu gods. I was deeply touched and gratified to see God use my testimony for such good.

I also brought along a small limestone from Jacob Creek. I wrote my family's names on the stone, and there, on the Andaman Islands, with several local pastors and villagers looking on intently, Pastor Simon read Psalm 46 in their native language. As he did, I kissed the stone and hurled it into the Indian Ocean as a point of release and closure. I felt a deeply powerful bond with those people because of our similar losses; they truly understood the devastating feeling of having lost loved ones in raging waters.

The foundation of my family's lives was our faith. And the foundation of our faith was Scripture. I had memorized dozens upon dozens of Scripture verses since I was 16. We had seen over and over in our lives that God's Word sustains us in the midst of trials. The trials we endured tested and strengthened our faith like a muscle. And our faith gave us the strength to persevere.

Since the dawn of time, God has done things that baffle humanity. He still confounds me. I don't know whether He intentionally took my family or whether He allowed them to die. I won't know this side of heaven. I can't control what happened, but I can control how I respond to what happened. It wasn't about what happened to me; it was about what happened *within* me.

I made a conscious, active decision to turn to God after the death of my family. It felt risky to willingly place my trust in a God who had seemingly just betrayed my entire lifetime of trust; it rebelled against every fiber of reasoning and logic in my being. It was one of the hardest things to do as a man. Yet in "losing" my life to God—giving Him absolute control—I regained it. In dying to myself, He gave me life again.

When we suffer great losses—and suffering and loss are universal experiences—something will consume our emptiness and fill the void. The question is, will it be healthy and wise or unhealthy and fleeting? I chose to be consumed by God. I found that only Christ could satisfy me. The pain was real and the healing process ongoing. I continued going to grief counseling, and I ate lots of peanut butter and ice cream!

But above and beyond all that, intimacy in God's presence—fellowship with Him—is what most healed my heart and restored my soul. It took faithful, intentional, and deliberate time every day to pray, read Scripture, worship, and wait patiently in God's presence. But every moment was worth it.

Scripture is filled with people who have suffered losses such as mine:

The word of the LORD came to me: "Son of man, with
one blow I am about to take away from you the delight of
your eyes." . . . So I spoke to the people in the morning,
and in the evening my wife died. The next morning I did
as I had been commanded. (Ezekiel 24:15–16, 18)

This verse feels like my life. Ezekiel embodied and epitomized
the consummate example of absolute trust, faith, and obedience to
God—regardless of what happens, regardless of what God requires.
Within one day, Ezekiel's wife—the delight of his eyes, his ultimate
sacrifice—was dead. Yet he didn't show any bitterness toward God,
even after being tasked with the thankless job of delivering countless
fire-and-brimstone messages to the disobedient Israelites.

In an instant, God took his most precious treasure just to deliver
a message to the people, just to make a point. Ezekiel paid such an
incredible price that not many would be willing to pay. He had every
human reason to be bitter and angry with God. He could have
tossed in the towel right then. But he didn't. He continued his
prophetic ministry without missing a beat.

I still believe God is a God of restoration and redemption. I
believe that when we shift our eyes from our own problems to God's
kingdom and caring for others, He will take care of the rest.

People often ask me how I can have such peace amid the enduring perpetual pain of missing my family. First, my heart is at peace
because I have no regrets—with God and with my family. My heart
is right with God. And I can look back on my family without regrets
because I cherished them while I could. I didn't live at the office. I
took quantity time with our children so we could uncover those rare
"quality" moments. I didn't live to work; I worked to live. I continued dating my wife even 13 years after we met.

We saw everyday life as something sacred and as a chance to make another memory. I don't suggest that we lived a perfect life. We had plenty of faults like any other family. But living without regrets meant that we lived our lives with a purpose: to make every day matter and to enjoy each other. We lived life like we meant it. We made every day count.

Second, the peace in my life is not mine. It is supernatural and superhuman. We aren't meant to understand it. If we could comprehend it, then it wouldn't be called a "peace [that] surpasses all understanding" (Philippians 4:7, NKJV). It's a gift from God. He freely gives it, but to do my part, I have to actively *accept* it.

I have learned that nothing can ever separate me from God's love. I know that even if everything that happens to me isn't good, God can still bring good out of everything. I have seen it in my life, and with my family—both before the flood and since then.

I don't understand fully how God's sovereignty and our free will blend together, and I never will until I get to heaven. But I do believe that our pain is sacred and that God has somehow ordained my suffering as something to shape me and transform me more into His image. Every ounce of suffering has a purpose that God can use for good, if we only let Him.

God clearly used the events of my life—childbirth, miscarriages, disabilities, international adoption, and many brushes with death—to forge and fortify my faith over the years. It occurred in the furnace of suffering. He groomed me to accept and handle an ordeal of mammoth proportions by His grace alone. His grace is always available, but I may not have been in the frame of mind to accept that grace had I not passed the other tests. Looking back, it's evident that it was clearly all a process.

But ultimately, I have to choose. I choose my attitude. On many mornings, it can be difficult. Yet I choose to be a victor, not a victim. I choose to be better, not bitter. I select life over death. I pick blessings over brokenness.

Over and over, Scripture commands me to trust in God, rejoice in Him, and be glad. That's not easy to do after devastating events and personal losses. Yet, since the flood, I have found that when I truly make my home in the presence of God Almighty—through daily Scripture reading, prayer, and worship—then I'm able to absolutely trust Him.

The words of King David summarize the stance of my heart and the posture of my soul—now, and from this day forward:

Whenever I am afraid,
I will trust in You.
In God (I will praise His word),
In God I have put my trust;
I will not fear.
What can flesh do to me? . . .

Put my tears into Your bottle;
Are they not in Your book? . . .

In God (I will praise His word),
In the LORD (I will praise His word),
In God I have put my trust;
I will not be afraid.
What can man do to me? . . .

I will render praises to You,
For You have delivered my soul from death.

Have You not kept my feet from falling,
That I may walk before God
In the light of the living?
(Psalm 56:3–4, 8, 10–13, NKJV)

Indeed, I will not be silent. I will sing to God and continue to give Him thanks, forever. For God is still good—all the time.

Epilogue

The names on the tombstones at Grandview Cemetery are hard to read now, after more than a century of exposure to the weather on the Kansas prairie. When the wind blows—and it almost always does in the Flint Hills—the rippling grass resembles gentle waves of a vast sea.

Robert Rogers traced the names of Martha and Edna May Jacobs with his fingers and felt a deep connection to them. They were killed in a flash flood at Jacob Creek in 1886, and Robert's wife and four children died in a flash flood at the same creek more than a century later.

Robert had visited the cemetery before, but this time he brought someone along: Inga, the waitress he first met only a few months after the tragedy. Nearly two years after first meeting, their friendship gradually blossomed into romance, and she wanted to learn more about his family and where they had been lost.

They walked along miles of Jacob Creek for hours, retracing his steps on that dreadful night and placing a rose for each member of his family at the precise location where they had been found by the search parties.

Robert and Inga exchanged marriage vows on May 20, 2006, in Fort Wayne, Indiana. As they travel the world together, telling this amazing testimony of faith, Inga embraces the place Melissa, Makenah, Zachary, Nicholas, and Alenah have in Robert's life.

"They will always be a part of him," she has said. "The more I know about them, the more I learn about Robert."

Robert is at peace. "Inga is truly a gift—heaven-sent."

As Romans 8:28 assures us, God can indeed bring good out of bad. He can redeem tragedy with new life . . . and new love.

"I am living proof," Robert says. "God is still a God of happy endings."

Notes

Prologue

1. *Chase County Leader*, May 13, 1886.
2. The Chase County Historical Society, comp., "The Cloudburst of May 6, 1886," *Chase County Historical Sketches*, vol. 2 (Cottonwood Falls, KS: Chase County Historical Society, 1948).

Chapter 7

1. Steven Curtis Chapman, "God is God," *Declaration*, copyright © 2001 by Sparrow Song.

Chapter 8

1. Horatio Spafford, "It Is Well with My Soul," copyright © 1873, public domain.

Chapter 20

1. Families with Children from China (FCC), "Frequently Asked Questions About Adoption from China: General Questions and Dossier Preparation Questions," March 10, 2002, http://www.fwcc.org,FAQ.htm.

Chapter 25

1. Dr. James and Shirley Dobson, *Night Light: A Devotional for Couples* (Sisters, OR: Multnomah, 2000), 12–13.

Chapter 27

1. Geron Davis, "We Are Standing (On Holy Ground)," copyright © 1983 by Meadowgreen Music.

Into the Deep
© Robert T. Rogers, 1994

Into the Deep, out of the shallow
Take me into the Light, out of the Shadows
Into the Deep, where Your river flows
I'll never know Your perfect will until I'm Into the Deep

Take a chance with the Messiah
Put His word to the test
Jump on in and He'll take care of the rest

Take your feet off the solid shore
Put your life into His hands
Take a leap of solid faith
Let His waters of love surround you when you're Into the Deep

AN INVITATION

If today were your last day on earth, would you have "no regrets" with God? Do you know for sure that you would go to heaven? Living a life of no regrets starts with knowing God personally. God loves you and wants you to have a close relationship with Him now and eternal life with Him in heaven:

> "For God so loved the world that he gave his one and only Son, that whoever believes in him shall not perish but have eternal life." (John 3:16)

But sin separates us from a holy God. To bridge that divide, God sent His only Son, Jesus Christ, to be the sacrifice for our sins. So choose life. Believe and accept God's free gift of salvation through His Son. It's as easy as A-B-C:

> *Admit you have sinned and need forgiveness.*
> "For all have sinned and fall short of the glory of God." (Romans 3:23)

> *Believe that Jesus died for you on the cross and then rose from the grave.*
> "But God demonstrates his own love for us in this: While we were still sinners, Christ died for us." (Romans 5:8)

> *Confess that Jesus Christ is your Lord, now and forevermore.*
> "If you confess with your mouth, 'Jesus is Lord,' and believe in your heart that God raised him from the dead, you will be saved." (Romans 10:9)

Just say a simple prayer like this:

Dear Jesus, I acknowledge the fact that I'm a sinner. I ask You to please forgive me. I believe You died for my sins and rose from the dead. I now turn away from all my sins and invite You to live in my heart. From this day forward, I want You to be the Lord of my life.

In Jesus' name. Amen.

If you said this prayer sincerely for the first time, congratulations! Welcome to God's family! Be sure to tell someone. You can call Focus on the Family at (800) A-FAMILY (232-6459) to share your news and pray with a member of the staff.

FREE Discussion Guide!
A discussion guide for *Into the Deep*
is available at

Mighty in the Land Ministry
Teaching Others to Live a Life of No Regrets

In response to continuing invitations for Robert to tell his story, he founded Mighty in the Land Ministry to help teach others to "live a life of no regrets" by knowing God personally first. Robert still travels the world and gives his testimony through music, Scripture, and vivid pictures. To order his inspiring music CDs or to schedule a life-changing ministry event, contact him at www.IntoTheDeep.org or by phone at 260.515.5158.

Mighty in the Land Foundation
Dedicated to advance adoption and care for orphans and special-needs children worldwide

"The Christian who is pure and without fault, from God the Father's point of view, is the one who takes care of orphans . . ." (James 1:27, TLB)

Robert has been led to do more than simply tell his story. In 2004, he established the Mighty in the Land Foundation to help disadvantaged children. In honor of his five family members, Robert's vision is to sponsor five orphanages in five regions of the world. Each will care for the children's physical, emotional, educational, medical, and spiritual needs. In October 2006, Robert dedicated the first orphanage: the "MELISSA HOME" Family Center in Russia's Vladimir region. A portion of this book's proceeds will help care for these orphans.

For more information on the Mighty in the Land Foundation and different ways you can contribute, visit www.IntoTheDeep.org or contact the foundation at:

Mighty in the Land Foundation
c/o Servant Christian Community Foundation
706 North Lindenwood Drive, Suite 100
Olathe, Kansas 66062
913.310.0279

FOCUS ON THE FAMILY®

Welcome to the Family ──

Whether you purchased this book, borrowed it, or received it as a gift, thanks for reading it! This is just one of many insightful, biblically based resources that Focus on the Family produces for people in all stages of life.

Focus is a global Christian ministry dedicated to helping families thrive as they celebrate and cultivate God's design for marriage and experience the adventure of parenthood. Our outreach exists to support individuals and families in the joys and challenges they face, and to equip and empower them to be the best they can be.

Through our many media outlets, we offer help and hope, promote moral values and share the life-changing message of Jesus Christ with people around the world.

Focus on the Family
MAGAZINES

These faith-building, character-developing publications address the interests, issues, concerns, and challenges faced by every member of your family from preschool through the senior years.

For More
INFORMATION

 ONLINE:
Log on to
FocusOnTheFamily.com
In Canada, log on to
FocusOnTheFamily.ca

 PHONE:
Call toll-free:
800-A-FAMILY
(232-6459)
In Canada, call toll-free:
800-661-9800

THRIVING FAMILY® Marriage & Parenting	**FOCUS ON THE FAMILY CLUBHOUSE JR.®** Ages 4 to 8	**FOCUS ON THE FAMILY CLUBHOUSE®** Ages 8 to 12	**FOCUS ON THE FAMILY CITIZEN®** U.S. news issues

Rev. 3/11

More expert resources
for marriage and parenting . . .

Do you want to be a better parent? Enjoy a stronger marriage? Focus on the Family's collection of inspiring, practical, resources can help your family grow closer and stronger than ever before. Whichever format you might need—video, audio, book or e-book, we have something for you. Visit our online Family Store and discover how we can help your family thrive at **FocusOnTheFamily.com/resources**.